The Citizen's Guide to Lobbying Congress

Donald E. deKieffer

CHICAGO
REVIEW
PRESS

Library of Congress Cataloging-in-Publication Data

DeKieffer, Donald E.
    The citizen's guide to lobbying Congress / by Donald E. deKieffer.
    — 1st ed.
        p.   cm.
    Includes bibliographical references (p.219) and index.
    ISBN 1–55652–194–4
    1. Lobbying—United States—Handbooks, manuals, etc.   I. Title.
JK1118.D425   1997
328.73'078—dc20   96–25644
                                                                                  CIP

First edition
Published by Chicago Review Press, Incorporated
814 North Franklin Street
Chicago, Illinois 60610

ISBN 1-55652-194-4
Printed in the United States of America

5 4 3 2 1

To Nancy,
for tolerating my
hours in the Black Hole

Contents

★ ★ ★ ★ ★

Foreword

★ ★ ★ ★ ★

—Congresswoman Patricia Schroeder, Democrat, of Colorado

In the eighteenth century, lobbyists were called "lobbiers" and were little more than merchants of greed. Lobbiers were denounced by everyone from Walt Whitman to President William McKinley. Mark Twain's novel *The Gilded Age* is about the venal Washington of the late 1800s.

Today there is more lobbying than ever, but the greed factor has been diluted by the rise in citizens' group lobbying, an altogether healthy trend in my view. The civil rights movement of the 1960s and the anti–Vietnam war movement of the 1970s, along with the pushes for a cleaner environment, open government, and Proposition 13 tax limitations, to cite just a few, are examples of citizen lobbying at work.

Mr. deKieffer's book is useful because it emphasizes the nuts and bolts, the dos and don'ts, for a successful lobbyist. Some may be put off by its nonideological tone. But that is its strength. Being prepared and well organized is a matter of technique, not ideology. *The Citizens Guide to Lobbying Congress* will prove particularly useful to the citizen lobbyists who cannot afford a phalanx of lawyers and public relations wizards. It's very much a how-to manual.

I must take exception, however, to some of his lobbying advice. Members of Congress don't all react the same way. In my office, for example, we don't allow people to buy our lunches. If you follow Mr. deKieffer's advice and your next lobbying campaign does not succeed, remember C. Northcote Parkinson: "Reform may be impossible, but we still (so far) have the right to laugh."

Foreword

★ ★ ★ ★ ★

**—Tom Korologos,
president of Timmons & Co.,
a Washington lobbying group, and
long-time friend and advisor to Bob Dole**

While some people decry the influence of special interests in Washington, the truth is that everyone has special interests that are represented in the halls of Congress—whether they know it or not. Teachers, bankers, environmentalists, and insect collectors are all represented by lobbyists on Capitol Hill who purport to speak for their constituencies.

Rather than decrying the existence of special interests, which, like sin and fat, will always be with us, individual citizens can use them to have an enormous impact on public policy. The trick is to understand the process.

Having been an observer and participant in the political process for three decades, I am constantly amazed at how effective some amateur lobbyists can be. They are generally not part of the Washington network and often lack the financial resources of their opponents, yet have won almost incredible victories. The record is replete with examples of citizen lobbyists defeating the supposed Goliaths of the special interests. The followers of George Wallace, Jesse Jackson, Pat Buchanan, the National Association of Women, the National Rifle Association, and Greenpeace understand this. This is what makes

American democracy so messy, inefficient, and vibrant. It was designed this way.

The Constitution was written by men who had an abiding distrust of government. They created a governmental structure with so many controls as virtually to assure that citizens would have a voice in the creation and execution of the laws. Since they (correctly) assumed that there would be a huge diversity of interests in the populace, this structure guaranteed that decisions would be taken with deliberation, and huge dollops of politics.

This is not to suggest that the rules of Washington are easy to understand. Many skilled politicians (including not a few who have risen to high office) have failed to appreciate the nuances of the Washington game. Nevertheless, armed with basic information and common sense, ordinary Americans do have a significant impact on the future of the Republic—not only in the voting booth, but in the daily deliberations of the Congress.

Whatever one's political predilections, participation in the government process can be a fascinating and rewarding experience. Armed with this basic text, and with the other sources cited in it, you and your neighbors can acquire as much influence as all but a few of the Washington insiders. Many members of Congress would wish this were not so.

Acknowledgments

The author gratefully acknowledges the assistance of Jack Nugent, one of the most professional lobbyists in Washington; Bill Reinsch, for his insights into the Hill staff system; Senator John Heinz, for his patience and advice; and Karen Porter, for her dedication and perseverance in reducing this manuscript to readable form.

One

★ ★ ★ ★ ★

So You Want to Be a Lobbyist

★ ★ ★ ★ ★

I have come to the conclusion that politics is too serious a matter to be left to the politicians.

—Charles de Gaulle

What Is Lobbying?

Outside of Washington, the business of lobbying is generally equated with all sorts of skulduggery. In the hustings, a lobbyist is about as highly regarded as a Mafia hit man or a crooked county sheriff. Quite frankly, lobbyists themselves have not done much to improve this image. Many actively promote the myth that lobbying requires some kind of special magic and that the successful practitioner must have a little black book filled with telephone numbers of women of dubious repute, paper bags full of unmarked bills, and twenty years' experience in the "old-boy" network of Washington professionals. Some Washington lobbyists intentionally perpetuate these myths to justify their own existence and to discourage do-it-yourselfers. Quite obviously, this book is not designed for them.

In the broadest sense, any time you write a letter to your congressman, or question a candidate at a political meeting, you are a lobbyist.

The definition of lobbying is one of the most controversial questions in the American political system. Our Constitution guarantees all citizens the unqualified right to petition their government for redress of grievances and the freedom to state their views without governmental interference. The dividing line between merely exercising a constitutionally guaranteed right and professional lobbying defies easy definition. The Congress and the courts have labored over this question on numerous occasions.[1] Perhaps Justice Potter Stewart's comment about pornography—you may not be able to define it but you know it when you see it—is also appropriate for lobbying. However vague the definition of lobbying in a practical sense, the laws regulating lobbying are very specific and must be complied with. They will be considered later in this chapter.

The History of Lobbying

Ever since human beings organized themselves into communities, the course of government policy has been influenced by lobbyists. Over the centuries, lobbyists have gone by different names and have, at times, camouflaged their true purpose by adopting official-sounding titles. A grand vizier of the thirteenth century was no less a lobbyist than the president of the National Coal Association is today. The Committees of Correspondence during the American Revolutionary period, although not an official part of the government, had an enormous impact upon the future of the Republic.

Although every country that is not totally anarchic allows some form of lobbying, it is only in the United States that this political phenomenon has been virtually institutionalized. This is due to two primary factors. The first is the structure of our constitutional system. The authors of the Constitution, perhaps overreacting to the lack of credence given their opinions by King George, guaranteed lobbyists a place in the American political system by inclusion of at least three provisions in the Constitution and the Bill of Rights protecting the freedom of interest groups to present their causes to the sovereign. These protections also were in conformity with the character of the American people. Alexis de Toqueville, in his writings about colonial and postcolonial America, was struck by the Yankee tendency

---

[1] Washington professionals are as sensitive about referring to the legislative body as "the" Congress and not merely "Congress" as are San Franciscans about not referring to their city as "San Fran" or "Frisco."

to form associations and pressure groups whenever two or more individuals discovered a shared interest.

The second factor that encouraged the development of lobbying in the United States was the structure of government itself. Congressmen—and later senators—were and are popularly elected. Although numerous philosophical studies and doctoral theses have been written about the function of members of Congress, the original and enduring reality has been that congressmen and senators serve to *represent* their constituencies first; their leadership obligations take second place.[2] The Founding Fathers strongly believed that the Congress was to serve as a check on the executive branch and not necessarily to provide the overall direction of the country.

Thus, armed with constitutional guarantees of freedom of expression, a political structure keyed to the parochial desires of different constituencies, and a basic cultural affinity for forming pressure groups, the concept of lobbying took strong and early root in the American political system. Although the term *lobbying* was not coined until several decades after the ratification of the Constitution, lobbyists were a vital part of the creation of that document itself. Both at the state and federal levels, lobbyists attempted (in many cases successfully) to condition accession of the states to specific protections for their own constituencies.

In the earliest days of the United States, lobbying began at the state level. The federal government concerned itself at that time with fewer issues of direct importance to a majority of Americans. The very term *lobbying* derived from the practice of state lobbyists pressing their causes in the corridors outside legislative chambers. Lobbyists, albeit to a lesser extent, were also present at the federal level, pressing their claims for federal shipbuilding contracts, supplying goods to government agencies, and arguing for central government assistance in suppressing Indian uprisings. A number of fascinating books have been written on the activities of these early lobbyists; a partial list is included in the Bibliography.

---

[2] Throughout this book, the terms *Congressman, Senator,* and *member of Congress* are used in the traditional Washington parlance; that is, *Congressman* is still used generically in preference to *Congressperson* and, I hope, does not signify any sexist tendencies on the part of the author. It refers specifically to a member of the House of Representatives.

Senator is quite obviously a member of the United States Senate, but as used in this book *member of Congress* is a member of either the House of Representatives or the Senate. Unless specifically indicated to the contrary, references to *the member* or *member of Congress* imply that the same lobbying techniques are equally applicable to either side of the Congress.

As the government became more complex, lobbyists became more specialized and sophisticated in their approach. Until the phenomenal growth of the congressional staffs in the early 1960s, lobbyists provided much of the political research for members of Congress and competed with Congressional Research Service (CRS), a branch of the Library of Congress, in supplying background data in support of (or in opposition to) proposed legislation.

Although it still seems sacrilegious to those outside the Washington Beltway, lobbyists actually have been writing much of the legislation of this country since its earliest days. Throughout most of the eighteenth and nineteenth centuries, however, the lobbyists' trade was practiced discreetly. There was little public disclosure of their activities and certainly no requirement for registration. This secrecy is partially responsible for the low esteem in which lobbyists generally are held today. "Influence peddling" has a long and sometimes unsavory history, and part of its mystique remains.

The underside of the lobbyist's craft was a subject of intense speculation and outright fabrication during the late nineteenth century. Like the dime novels that glamorized the American West, the role of the lobbyist was a subject of lurid speculation by newspapers and fiction writers of the time. Exposés of lobbyists for the great capitalist institutions continued well into the twentieth century. Lobbyists were characterized as little better than panderers and blackmailers, suborning public officials for their own greedy ends. Titillating stories written about methods used by these scoundrels rarely failed to include references to the use of wine and women in promoting their schemes—almost always to the detriment of the Republic.

Public outrage did not come like a thunderclap as in the case of Watergate, but rather through a growing sense of revulsion at the perceived evils of graft and corruption spawned by lobbyists. Early on, there was talk of banning lobbyists entirely; but even though public outrage was intense, an outright ban on lobbying faced insurmountable constitutional hurdles.

On the theory that corruption does not flourish in the sunshine, Congress did succeed in passing some disclosure laws regulating lobbying activities. Timid as these early laws appear by today's standards, they were a step forward in legitimizing lobbying. Even at a time of flagrant abuses of the most commonly accepted norms of conduct, most lobbyists' functions were informational rather than seditious in nature. The mere fact that lobbyists' identities were to be revealed had a salutary effect. To this day, many lobbyists object to fuller disclosure of their activities, but the objections are primarily based upon the nuisance of complying with reams of government regulations rather than a guilty conscience about untoward conduct. Reasonable disclosure requirements have, over the years, significantly reduced speculation about what lobbyists really do and what some members of the news media would like to have the public believe.

There is a fine line, however, between reasonable disclosure and harassment to the point where citizens are virtually forbidden to petition their own government for legitimate purposes. Some of the proposals by so-called public interest groups in the mid-seventies, for example, would have made almost all those who wrote to their congressmen potential lobbyists, subject to civil and criminal sanctions if they did not register. Other public interest groups, including Ralph Nader's Congresswatch, saw such proposals as an implicit threat to what they regarded as fundamental First Amendment guarantees. Most of the extreme proposals have since been defeated, but the state of the law with regard to lobbying is still unsettled.

Laws Regulating Lobbying

The original law regulating the activity of lobbyists dates back to 1946 (60 Stat. 839 [Aug. 2, 1946]). The Federal Regulation of Lobbying Act is basically a "sunshine law" that requires disclosure of lobbyists' activities, their principals, and the amounts they are paid. This law was significantly expanded by the adoption of the Lobbying Disclosure Act of 1995. (The full text of this law can be found in the Appendix.) Currently lobbyists are required to report on a semiannual basis to the clerk of the House of Representatives and the secretary of the Senate. The information requested is a rather complete disclosure of monies received and a full description of activities. Copies of the regulations as well as relevant provisions of the law and sample forms, are available from the clerk's and secretary's office. Since the law is constantly changing in this area, the lobbyist should be sure to check with the clerk for a copy of current regulations. Both the forms themselves and the instructions pertaining to them can be changed at any time.

Far more complex regulations apply in the case of lobbyists for foreign principals. The Foreign Agents Registration Act (52 Stat. 631 [June 8, 1938]) requires an explicit listing of all political activities undertaken by a lobbyist on behalf of any foreign principal. The definition of "foreign principal" includes both governmental and nongovernmental clients. Unless you are acting in a strictly legal capacity (exclusively as legal counsel to the foreign principal) you may be subject to this act. Failure to register and report on a semiannual basis to the Department of Justice can lead to severe criminal and civil sanctions. The Department of Justice regularly publishes booklets on the requirements of the Foreign Agents Registration Act. For more current information regarding the status of this act, write to the Foreign Agents Registration Section, Criminal Division, United States Department of Justice, Washington, D.C. 20530.

Despite some adverse publicity received by the Foreign Agents Registration Section, you will generally find them hard-nosed and helpful.

Lobbying As a Vital Part of the American Political System

Despite infrequent exposés of abuse, lobbying remains one of the best protections our country has against extremism. A Newtonian law of politics might be that every political cause will ultimately engender an equal and opposite cause. If competing philosophies are allowed to meet—not just in the marketplace of ideas but in the reality of legislation—we will ultimately protect the system itself from zealotry. Our constitutional system has built-in delays that permit the formation of groups to support legislation they approve or oppose legislation that they feel would be inimical to their beliefs. "Decree laws," so familiar in many other countries and adopted without consultation with competing groups, are totally alien to the American system and tend to foment radical rather than gradual change.

The term *special interest group,* like the word *lobbyist,* has attracted a kind of reprobation in recent years that is altogether undeserved. Every citizen is a special interest who must be considered in the process of adopting the law of the land. Blacks, consumers, teachers, proabortionists, gun control advocates, handicapped people, aliens, exporters, salesmen—all are special interests whose views deserve cognizance. There is not an American today who is not represented (whether knowingly or not) by at least a dozen special interest groups. Rather than decry the legitimacy of special interest groups, they should be recognized for what they are: the grassroots of the American political process. Not only is lobbying an honorable profession, it is probably one of the most important in our society.

On a personal level, lobbyists can derive an immense amount of satisfaction from knowing that they have helped shape the political, social, and even moral foundation of this country. In short, lobbying is no more a dirty business than any other profession. Although it has its share of hounders, so do the medical, legal, and stockcar-driving professions. This is not to excuse malfeasance among those who lobby: they have a special trust, and the stakes are simply too high to permit license for those who would abuse it.

Two

★ ★ ★ ★ ★

What's the Issue?

★ ★ ★ ★ ★

Politics, n. Strife of interests masquerading as a contest of principles.

—Ambrose Bierce

Single-Issue Lobbies

In the past decade, there has been a remarkable transformation in the American political system. Although party platforms have always had planks on issues ranging from national defense to farm policy, and special interest groups have traditionally played a role in the development of these planks, it is only in recent years that single-issue groups have had the enormous impact on public policy that they have today.

Formerly, political parties and even candidates attempted to base their campaigns on what they felt were the attitudes of a majority of the voters on various issues. While no one group would be completely satisfied by a given candidate or party, a carefully planned "consensus approach" virtually guaranteed moderation on most issues, whatever the candidate's partisan label. All this has changed in the past few years. Special interest groups have learned that their electiveness is directly proportional to their willingness to base their votes on a single issue. Whatever else a candidate may do, that candidate must vote with these special interest groups on individual items or face loss of their support, whether or not they agree with the candidate on other issues.

This trend prevails particularly with some of the more emotional topics—environmental issues, abortion rights, gun control, and so forth. While there is considerable debate about whether the trend toward stronger single-issue lobbies bodes well for the traditional moderation of the American system, few informed commentators would deny that it has become a significant factor in electoral politics. The rise of the single-issue lobby has also involved many more people in the legislative process. The power of special interest groups has been enhanced by their willingness to use their political muscle, and their lobbying techniques have become sophisticated. Single-issue lobbies do not have to trade off gains for their cause against other political considerations; in fact, they often have nothing to give.

In former years, and to some extent today, congressmen attempted to balance conflicting interests by voting for projects most of their constituents would like most of the time. This gave the members the freedom to take controversial stands on particular issues without fear of losing their seat because of one or two unpopular votes. That freedom has now been diminished by the special interest lobbies.

As with most phrases regarding lobbying, "single issue" is also deceptive. No knowledgeable person would suggest that proponents of the Equal Rights Amendment are lobbying for a single issue: the implications of the women's rights movement go far beyond the mere adoption of a constitutional amendment. Even gun control advocates do not see themselves in a position of a single-issue lobby: dozens of laws and social policies would be affected if they were successful in their campaign. "Single issue," as used here, is meant only to distinguish broad-based associations and trade unions that consider dozens of unrelated legislative topics simultaneously from more parochial groups that concentrate on one aspect of government policy.

While editorial writers and so-called reformers decry the very existence of what they brand special interests, nothing could be more traditionally American than the promotion of various ideas through combined effort. Indeed, most of those who condemn the special interests are special interests themselves. John Gardner's Common Cause, the various Nader groups, and even the *Washington Post* have clearly defined vested interests for which they aggressively lobby. While the objectives of various special interest groups may vary, the fact of their parochial objectives is manifest.

Some groups purport to represent the "public interest" to distinguish themselves from the allegedly selfish goals of their opponents. Although such a label undoubtedly provides good copy for the media, and many public interest groups' members honestly believe that they are promoting the common good, it is clear that not all citizens share their values. One person's public interest is another person's despotism; the mere label does not make it so. Is it more in the public interest to increase park land at the expense of industrial development or to create jobs for minorities at the expense of the environment? These are public interest *questions*, not public interest answers.

This is not to suggest that these self-styled public interest groups do not serve a valuable function, but merely that there is virtually no lobbying group—no matter how it may choose to label itself—that is not a special interest. Thus, the debate about the perceived evils of special interests is largely an exercise in polemics. Whatever goals your group espouses, merely recognize that you *are* one of the special interests. There is nothing wrong with this; indeed, as stated earlier special interest lobbying is at the heart of the American political system. Citizen participation in government should be encouraged rather than condemned as some sleazy practice of the privileged. The purpose of this book is to enable more special interests to participate in the political process.

Multiple-Issue Lobbies

Although, as noted above, special interest groups have proliferated over the past decade, the most powerful lobbies in Washington still remain multiple interests such as labor unions, business organizations, and trade associations. These groups have traditionally tended to be flexible in their approach to politics. At any given time they may be working on a dozen different pieces of legislation that could affect their members in different ways. They are thus much more likely to accept compromise to achieve their overall goals. For example, a trade union may reluctantly back away from a hard stand on an international trade issue to gain votes on minimum-wage legislation.

To do this successfully, the large multiple-issue lobbies must be highly sophisticated. Often their lobbying activities are tightly controlled by a legislative director with years of experience in the art of compromise and political "hardball." To the extent that multiple-issue lobbies do not have this kind of control, they tend to be crushed by their own diversity. Either they fight every issue with equal ferocity or they give up on the verge of victory, thus squandering their power.

Size alone rarely determines a group's political effectiveness. The larger a group becomes, the more difficult it is to control. Some of the largest industrial trade associations in the country have dismal records of success in lobbying, whereas some smaller groups and unions have admirable batting averages.

Growth itself sometimes makes larger associations less powerful. As an association becomes more diverse, the likelihood of internal controversy becomes greater. Such controversy is not only philosophic but economic. For example, industrial trade unionists may oppose imported products as threats to their jobs; but retail clerks who sell both foreign and domestic goods may believe that imports keep prices down, thus increasing consumer spending and creating a greater need for *their* jobs.

The same dichotomies occur in industrial organizations and even in so-called public interest groups that attempt to broaden their membership. A striking example of this has been the debate over the fate of wild burros in the Grand Canyon. Some environmentalists charge that the burros were not indigenous to the area and have destroyed much of the native flora; others argue that destroying the burros is fundamentally antihumanitarian and are appalled at suggestions that the burros be annihilated for the sake of grass.

Thus, although the multiple-issue lobbies are by far the largest in Washington (and most would agree are still the most powerful), the growth of single- or restricted-issue organizations in recent years is testimony to the fact that the huge trade unions and business groups do not have a monopoly on the course of legislative affairs.

Identifying the Issue

To most novice lobbyists, it seems almost presumptuous to suggest that they have not defined the issue they want to support or oppose. Yet one of the reasons most lobbying campaigns fail is that the lobbyists do not have a firm grasp of either the primary or ancillary issues involved in their campaign. Even the most apparently straightforward political issue may have legal and social repercussions that a novice would not foresee. The most laudable goals (such as the prevention of cancer) have been met by controversy because well-intentioned promoters did not fully understand the issues involved. They should have realized, for example, that a law banning *any* cancer-causing substance might ultimately wind up prohibiting all sorts of delicacies relished by the American public and, if enforced, could damage the credibility of the lawmakers themselves.

There has never been a political objective desired by *any* group that did not have effects beyond the stated objective of the sponsors. This fact further clouds the definition of "single-issue lobbies." There is no such thing as a single-issue political goal. By the very nature of politics, there will always be a number of issues. This being the case, adequate homework must be done before any actual lobbying in the field is undertaken.

Three

★ ★ ★ ★ ★

Homework

★ ★ ★ ★ ★

Laws are inherited like diseases.
—Johann Wolfgang von Goethe

Research on the Issue

No matter how clever you perceive your group members to be, inevitably someone has already thought of any ideas you have. There is little satisfaction in reinventing the wheel, so your first obligation should be to spend a lot of time in the library. As noted in Chapter 2, your research should consider not only factual and philosophical justifications for your position, but also the effects its institutionalization would have on other issues.

For the purposes of this book (and to avoid belittling any current ideologies), we will follow the planning and execution of a lobbying campaign launched by the Flat Earth Society (FES), a mythological beast whose mission is to promote the cubic nature of the planet and to stamp out the heresy of round earthism. The scenario is as follows: the Flat Earth Society has chapters in twenty-six states and the District of Columbia, with twenty-seven hundred active members. Although it has been engaged in a number of legislative battles over the years, it is now facing its greatest challenge. A bill has been introduced in the House of Representatives that would not only ban the teaching of flat earth theory in public schools, but also provide federal funds to promote the concept that the planet is a sphere. This, of course, strikes at the very heart of flat earth theology, and the society is geared up to turn back this assault.

Initially, flat earth researchers have undertaken to discover all other issues. The following is their preliminary list:

1. The proposed legislation would increase government spending and thus inflation.

2. Possible constitutional questions would be raised regarding the freedom of speech and religion.

3. The federal bureaucracy would be increased to administer the program.

4. The time spent on round earth instruction would take away time from teaching basic courses (such as mathematics and reading) to the detriment of minorities.

5. Teachers might support round earthism as increasing the number of teachers' jobs.

6. The mapmakers' position is unknown: they might need to make new maps if the flat earth theory were accepted.

7. The defense establishment would probably argue that round earth theory is "advanced technology." They would likely contend that instruction in this "science" is necessary to maintain military parity with potential adversaries.

8. Federal standards of instruction for primary schools would undermine the authority of local school boards to set curriculum. Thus, school boards might be allies of the Flat Earth Society.

9. Since flat earth maps are different from round earth maps, surveying changes could affect boundaries of large properties, such as farms. The net political effect is unknown.

10. International navigation rules would have to be altered to reflect whichever theory prevails, thus creating the possibility of foreign policy problems.

11. This is another example of federal government intrusion into private lives—today round earth, tomorrow Big Brother.

Although many of the examples listed above may appear ludicrous to individuals with common sense, they are exactly the types of unrelated questions raised in actual lobbying campaigns. If it is a heavily contested effort, you can be certain that apparently absurd (or at least imaginative) issues will be discussed during the course of the debate. It is best if you can identify as many of these as possible *before* you start your campaign and be thoroughly briefed before you announce your group's intentions. Members of Congress and congressional staffs have an uncanny knack for asking such questions as how your proposal would affect the fishing catch in the Bering Sea and giving you five reasons why it could. You had best know the answers before you are asked the questions.

Know Your Enemies

One of the greatest mistakes you can make as a lobbyist is to assume that, merely because your opponents disagree with you, they are a pack of scoundrels and idiots. Particularly on emotional issues, it is sometimes difficult to acknowledge that your opponents have a cumulative intelligence quota of more than two digits. After all, if they were so smart, they would be able to see the merit of your views. Unfortunately, they probably feel the same way about you.

The best thing to do is to find out as much as possible about your opponents: who they are, who supports them, and what their arguments are. A good first step is to get your hands on as much of their propaganda as possible—pamphlets, books, newspaper articles; anything in which they have made a public statement should be reviewed by your research committee. This will give you a good initial idea of the types of arguments you can expect to get on the Hill. It may be that you have identified some issues that your opponents have not recognized, but you should first be sure you can persuasively rebut the arguments they believe are important.

Try to identify groups that have joined your opponents or could be expected to sympathize with the views they espouse. Again, you should speculate about groups whose interests would seem to be best served by siding with your opponents and who may not have done so. It is better to anticipate the worst than to be surprised later.

According to the mythology of lobbying, your next step would be to get involved in behind-the-scenes groping for personal "dirt" on the leadership of your opposition. This, however, is not only tasteless; it is amateurish. Despite a few exceptional cases, personal peccadilloes do not have much effect on the Washington scene. Even raising such issues as your opponent's love life can be counterproductive: people on the Hill might be bemused or even titillated by spicy revelations, but they will hardly respect you or your position for publicizing them.

The exception to this rule is when you can conclusively demonstrate that your opponents have either lied or substantially misrepresented their true objectives. For example, proof that a so-called environmentalist group is being secretly funded by polluting industries might warrant revelation under certain circumstances. *Warning:* if you come across information of this nature, don't get "buck fever." Settle down; check your facts again; check your *own* closet for skeletons; and take very, very careful aim before squeezing the trigger. Your credibility is at stake as much as your opponents'. If you make unsubstantiated claims about them, you will suffer more than they.

Just because you have identified another group as a potential opponent, don't write it off until it has actually taken action against you. You don't want any more enemies than necessary, and it is sometimes possible to neutralize potential opponents by judicious compromise. Even when you have positively identified your opponents, do not sell them short. The greatest mistake you can make is to underestimate the intelligence, fortitude, and commitment of those who disagree with you.

One final note: it is almost always a bad idea to pull a stunt like planting an informant in your opponent's camp. The informant could be discovered, and you would almost certainly be exposed for this kind of skulduggery; if you are exposed, your credibility will plummet and your entire campaign may be lost (remember Watergate); and it is highly unlikely you would discover anything from such a maneuver that you could not gain by diligent scholarship. With the stakes as high as they are, it makes little sense to risk the entire program for a juvenile attempt at espionage.

This is not to say your opponents might not be tempted to try spying. The best protection you have from this is not stiff security measures, but your own integrity. The only useful information your opponents could discover by infiltrating your operation would be on some off-the-wall stunt you yourself may be planning. Fight hard and fight clean. That's not moralizing, it's practical. If you have the facts and credibility, you have the battle half won.

Know Your Friends

Most successful lobbying campaigns spend more time and energy cultivating friends than denouncing enemies. As with identification of the issues, identification of friends is extremely important. If there are any groups that could be affected by your position (there will be dozens), contact them. You can broaden your influence far beyond the membership of your group if you can legitimately claim the endorsement of other organizations. Better yet, these groups can lend you time, money, manpower, and expertise that may be otherwise unavailable to you.

You will have to face reality about political "friends": they may be with you today and against you tomorrow, so do not sell your soul. In politics, alliances are for convenience, not love. Notwithstanding the transient nature of political friendships, they are indispensable in lobbying.

The first thing you should recognize about potential friends is that they rarely volunteer. You must give them a good reason for helping. In fact, you will probably spend as much time lobbying your allies as you will the Hill. "Keep your troops in line" is the most important and most frequently disregarded axiom of lobbying. Organizations whose members are politically experienced will not join you for philosophical reasons; you will have to show them very specific ways your issue will benefit them. You will also have to remind them of promises they have made regarding their support. Undying oaths of friendship carry little practical weight; you will have to spend as much time giving backbone transfusions to your allies as you do in the political trenches on Capitol Hill. To the uninitiated this can be a frustrating and disillusioning experience. Promises will be broken, personal vendettas begun, and outright treason committed; but you are still best served by having allies. Toughen your hide and sharpen your tongue. It's hard to live with them, but you can't live without them.

On the other hand, your group will probably also be approached by others seeking help. Rules to follow in such a situation are:

1. Make sure it is in your group's interest to support the proposal itself. *Never* agree to an alliance merely because you believe the group making the request could be valuable to you at some future date. Lobbyists tend to have very short memories.

2. *Never* make promises you cannot, or do not intend to, keep. You should be very specific about what you will and will not do and vague about areas you wish to consider. *Never* leave the other group with the impression you promised something that you didn't. Your credibility is as important with your allies as it is with congressmen.

In your search for friends, you should base your decisions on issues presented—not the general philosophical inclination of your potential allies. Politics makes strange bedfellows. Some of the most successful lobbying groups in recent memory have been composed of such traditionally antagonistic forces as labor and management (in international trade law); conservative Westerners and environmentalists (conservation issues); religious cults and the Eastern press (First Amendment questions); and Communists and energy companies (nuclear power). Don't let initial distaste govern common sense in forming temporary alliances with generally inimical groups. This is hardball politics, not a college debating society. However philosophically removed you may be from an ally in general political persuasion, the credibility of your campaign can be enhanced by bringing together apparently disparate groups. Swallow your prejudices and do it.

The ground rules of these fragile alliances should be very clearly set out. Don't attempt to bait your ally on issues unrelated to the problem at hand. All that will breed is suspicion and dissension. Don't expect to turn around your newfound friends on every matter, but be sure you don't compromise on any issue unrelated to the project at hand.

What's the Law?

You may conceive of your group as more concerned about policy than legal technicalities, but if you are involved in lobbying, your ultimate objective is to change the provisions of existing statutes. It is not enough to say you want clean water or even the Walnut Creek cleaned up. Your group's real objective is to amend Section 14(b)(2)(ii). Whether you like it or not, you must enter the shadowy world of lawyers. You must not only know the general objectives of your project, but how the new law should *technically* read. This is not just a lobbying tactic. Remember, clever lawyers representing your opponents will probably take the new law to court. If you have made any errors, or your intent is unclear, they will tie the statute in knots for years to come.

If you are not a lawyer, the best way to determine the status of the current law and the way you would like it to be is to request a legal memorandum (*not* an opinion letter) from an experienced law firm. If you decide to do this, be sure to agree *in advance* on the approximate cost of such a project. Law firms make a great deal of money from open-ended assignments. Although it can be a significant expense, a legal memorandum on the interpretation of the law is indispensable. To paraphrase Congressman Michael Myers, convicted of bribery in the Abscam investigation, "Specifics talk, bullshit walks." There is no substitute for a carefully researched analysis of the way current law has been interpreted by the courts and a cross-check on other laws that would be affected by implementation of your position. This analysis should be done very early in any lobbying campaign. Although it appears to merely create work for lawyers, it is ultimately a bargain. If you fail to get sound legal advice at the outset, you are almost guaranteed to pay ridiculous fees to correct the problems that will arise later.

Who Are the Players?

Once you have recognized friends, enemies, and the status of the law, you need to locate the individuals on the Hill who will consider your issue.

When legislation is introduced in either the House or the Senate, it is immediately referred to a committee. Although the committee structure is rather complex (see Chapter 11), you should be able to determine which committee and subcommittee will consider your bill. Once you know this, you can start making your list of congressional contacts. First list all appropriate committee and subcommittee members (by party) and all the members of the House Rules Committee (the Rules Committee considers almost all legislation at one point or another). Next list the names of all congressmen and senators traditionally on your side of the issue. You can get a general idea of their voting patterns by reviewing the *Almanac of American Politics* and seeing which ones have voted on similar issues in the past. This information is also available in greater detail from the House and Senate policy committees, which have computerized analyses of all "record votes." Finally, there are numerous sources on the Internet that can provide valuable information. A partial list of particularly interesting web sites is included in Chapter 19.

Finally, you should categorize every member on your list according to your access to them; that is, do you have constituents in their state or district? Do any of your members know any of the congressmen or their staffs on a personal basis? Would the legislation have an immediate effect upon the congressmen's or senators' districts?

From this analysis you should prepare an outline of all possible contacts with members of Congress who might consider your bill. List every access route to each congressman who will be exposed to your legislation in committee or subcommittee; then determine how best to approach them either through your own members or the allies you have cultivated.

At this stage it is also important to recognize the administrative agency that will be charged with enforcing the legislation with which you are concerned. Without the administrative agency's agreement, it is likely that the executive branch will actively oppose you on the Hill. The administration can field more lobbyists than you can, and it is essential that you at least neutralize its opposition.

Because the government has grown so complex, it is a virtual certainty that more than one agency will be affected by any piece of legislation. Therefore, you should look not only to the primary but also to the other departments and bureaus that would be touched by your project. The legal memorandum mentioned earlier should help you do this. You should ask your attorneys to include this as part of their assignment.

Contrary to popular opinion, the government is not a monolith. Agencies are as jealous of their own prerogatives as private special interest groups. Even if the agency charged with the primary responsibility for administering the legislation you propose is opposed to your position, don't give up hope. Some other agency is almost certain to support you because of its institutional hatred of the "primary" agency. Be sure to list *all* such government agencies in your initial chart of "friends"; approach them early in the lobbying campaign.

The support of a given agency does not necessarily mean that the executive branch will condone your position, but open disagreement among the various branches of government can effectively hamstring organized opposition to your point of view. If you think the agency that would ordinarily be charged with administering your program would be hostile to your position, it may be wise to sow the seeds of dissension among competing agencies. For example, an environmental bill may have an impact upon programs of the Department of Defense (strategic materials, military reservations, defense contractors, and so on), the Department of Labor (lost jobs), and the Department of Energy (development of new energy sources).

Allies within the administration can also be a valuable source of information with regard to interagency bickering. They can give you an unsurpassed advantage if you can convince them to issue reports supporting your position, even if the ultimate decision of the administration is to oppose you. Most agencies have the legal authority to publish studies, "white papers," and so on that may not conform to the "administration line." These have often been successfully used on the Hill to undercut the official position of the administration. Since official government studies are given great credence on the Hill, any time you spend with administrative agencies is well invested.

The Resource Book

Once you have completed your homework, it must be organized into a usable format. The resource book will be your bible throughout the lobbying campaign. It is best to set this up in a three-ring, loose-leaf notebook, tab-indexed to various subjects. A sample format is as follows:

Existing Law

Photocopies of existing federal statutes, tab-indexed, pertinent sections highlighted or underlined.

Legal Memoranda

Legal memoranda prepared by your attorneys as described in this chapter.

Opponents

Addresses, telephone numbers, and leadership; photocopies of sample propaganda they have distributed regarding your subject.

Allies

Addresses and telephone numbers; narrative descriptions of the subissues about which your allies are particularly concerned. It is important to include the names of as many contact persons, both in Washington and in the field, as possible.

Congressional Contacts

Include all members of Congress who will have direct contact with your measure on a committee level, as well as known congressional allies and opponents. These should each be separately tab-indexed. Include each relevant congressman's name, office address, telephone number, complete staff, congressional district map, biography, and a list of constituents in his or her district with whom you have direct contact.

Administrative Agencies

All administrative agencies that would be affected by your proposal should be listed together with a narrative description of their position vis-à-vis your issue. You should list names, addresses, and telephone numbers of all contacts in the agency so you can communicate with them rapidly.

Issues

List various issues that could be raised during the course of the debate on your proposed legislation. The issues, and your views on them, should be stated succinctly. This section is the most important of the entire resource book and is the "party line" you will expect your members to follow when questioned. It must be very carefully edited and proofread, and should incorporate every issue you can conceive of. This section should be heavily footnoted with sources of your information and should include charts, statistics, and so on upon which your argument relies.

The resource book is a very sensitive document and should not be widely distributed, even among members of your own group. You should institute several controls to limit distribution, including marking each copy with a control number. These control numbers should be assigned to specific people within your organization, who then should be charged with maintaining confidentiality. With the exception of the issues section, the resource book should *not* be taken to the Hill during your contacts with congressional offices.

Although putting together a resource book may seem rather painstaking work, the time spent in carefully researching your issue and making sure your supporters understand it is worthwhile. If you have done your job properly, you will not have to do additional research on questions that arise during the course of a campaign; you will have considered them already. In short, the resource book is the document most valuable to a lobbyist's campaign.

Four

★ ★ ★ ★ ★

The Action Plan

★ ★ ★ ★ ★

General good is the plea of the scoundrel, hypocrite, and flatterer.

—William Blake, *Jerusalem*

You have finished your research; identified your issues, your friends, and your enemies; but it is still not time to attack the Hill. First you must develop a *thorough* plan for implementing the research you have already done. The action plan is your procedural guide for the entire campaign. As with the resource book, it will be a highly confidential document and should be distributed only to those in your group directly involved with actual lobbying. The best action plans are the product of several people's thinking, so share your ideas with others in your group. It is generally best, however, not to attempt to write an action plan in a committee meeting but rather to circulate drafts among your members and work out details together later.

The action plan is more than a calendar of events of your campaign; it is quite literally your line of battle, and it includes schedules, names of the players, and the method by which you will implement your entire strategy. Like the resource book, the action plan should be in a three-ring, loose-leaf binder so that changes can be easily made. The precise content of each section will be dealt with in subsequent chapters.

Press Relations

How members of the press perceive your lobbying campaign is crucial. Your relations with the media will be especially important if your program is controversial. Therefore, be particularly sensitive to the issues described in Chapter 5. The action plan regarding press relations should include press contacts, clearance procedures, congressional contacts, letters, demonstrations, gimmicks, and the Hill blitz.

Press Contacts

Specify all persons authorized to speak to the press. Unfortunately, many organizations have more press spokesmen than they have members. Since the media constitute one of your most important means of communicating your views to the public, it is essential that only one or two be authorized to speak for your group to the press. All others should refer inquiries to the press-contact personnel. Although this may appear to be an undemocratic or oppressive policy, the media are fond of exploiting internal dissension by extemporaneous interviews. The worst thing you can do is to permit everyone to represent your group's views to the public. The press relations section of your action plan should explicitly list the names of the individuals authorized to state your views.

The press contacts section should also include the names, addresses, and telephone numbers of reporters for publications that have an interest in your issue. The *News Media Yellow Book*, listed in Chapter 19, provides this information. These individuals should be included in your press release list and should receive hand-delivered or faxed copies of press releases as they become available. Your press contacts list should not include every reporter or publication listed in the *News Media Yellow Book*, only those with whom you have a reasonable working relationship. If you would like to include others, be sure to indicate those individuals with whom you have personal contact by an asterisk or some other symbol.

Clearance Procedures

This section of your action plan should describe in detail the procedures you intend to follow when issuing statements to the media.

Generally, it is best if only one person be designated to prepare press statements. These draft statements, however, should always be reviewed by at least two other high-ranking persons in your group. Procedures should be outlined as to how such clearances should be accomplished. Most news items have a time value, so you should not wait for a formal meeting, but establish a protocol for approving the releases over the telephone.

Few issues can lead to more acrimony within a group than unauthorized press releases. Members of your group deserve all the information made available to the press *before* the media are advised. The clearance methodology should be agreed on in advance by as many people as possible, but the procedure itself should be rather simple. Three—at most four—individuals should be given sole discretion to make decisions. By the time a large committee meeting could be called and the issues discussed, the news value of a press release could be diminished or destroyed.

In all your press releases you should include contact persons who can answer additional questions. These people should be the same individuals authorized to clear the original press release. Within your group you should discuss the nature and extent of additional information these contact persons are authorized to disclose. Although you cannot anticipate every question the press might ask (they are geniuses at embarrassing queries), you should have some general guidelines. To be sure that all answers to press inquiries are consistent, your spokesman should parrot the information contained in the resource book. Aside from general information about your group's membership, it is rarely advisable to comment on questions regarding the internal politics of your organization. Press speculation about internal differences of opinion makes good copy, but it also guarantees dissension. The rule when answering such questions is to refuse to speculate. If absolutely necessary, you can put the best slant on any problems you have, noting (with a straight face) that "the diversity of views in our group is our strength."

Congressional Contacts

This is one of the most complex sections of your action plan and, as such, should be extensively annotated and cross-indexed. The format of this section can vary according to the needs of your group but should include at least the following:

1. Names, addresses, and telephone numbers of key members of the Congress, particularly those assigned to committees that will be considering your matter.

2. Names, addresses, and telephone numbers of members of Congress with whom your group has exceptionally good relations, particularly in those districts where your organization is strong, whether or not those congressmen sit on the committees directly affected by your issue.

3. Staff contacts both on committees and personal staffs. This is extremely important (see Chapter 11). The staff list should include their personal telephone numbers and the contacts you have already made. The list should include any further details about each staff member's background that are relevant.

4. Congressional demographics. You should prepare a complete demographic sketch of each member of Congress whom you list, including a congressional district map, and an analysis of his or her district (see *The Almanac of American Politics*, listed in Chapter 19). You should also include an analysis of any constituent relationships your group may have with the member.

5. Complete analysis of all congressmen mentioned and their voting records on similar issues. These are available from the various Senate and House Policy Committees and on the Internet (see Chapter 19).

6. Incidental information about ancillary groups' influence on individual members and the method by which members may be approached through such groups.

Letters

Your action plan should contain a section devoted to letter-writing assignments. This should be organized according to constituent relationships with the congressional contacts listed above. Letters should be composed according to the outline in Chapter 6. The letter-writing section of the action plan should contain a sample format of letters to the Hill and a check-off list. Photocopies of all letters sent to the Hill should be forwarded to your group's headquarters or a committee established for this purpose. It will be responsible for assuring compliance with the letter-writing assignments. This committee should also be responsible for preparing responsive letters to congressmen for further information or to correct errors. Such follow-up letters should be signed by the constituent directly involved; members of the drafting committee should not respond to the congressman on their own initiative.

All this might seem a rather elaborate system for putting a few words down on paper, but more lobbying campaigns have been ruined by friends than by enemies. As some contemporary politicians have shown us, it is quite easy to shoot yourself in the foot in Washington; the best way to avoid this is to keep the safety on, even when it involves a little more effort.

Demonstrations

As you will see in Chapter 7, demonstrations are rarely as effective as a well-planned lobbying campaign. Get your members off the streets and into the halls of the Congress where they can make a much greater impact. Demonstrations are sometimes the only alternative, however, when you have a large, loosely structured cause and it is impossible to effectively direct the activities of your membership. This is the case particularly when you have uncontrollable fringe elements who will not agree to a coordinated plan. In that event it is sometimes better to keep them *away* from members of Congress; they can do more to confuse the issue than to clarify it. If, for whatever reason, you decide that a demonstration is necessary or desirable, it should be very carefully planned.

The demonstrations section of your action plan should include at least the following:

1. Date, time, and place of the demonstration.

2. Names, addresses, and telephone numbers of groups expected to participate in the demonstration, together with names of the leaders of such groups.

3. Names, addresses, and telephone numbers of all public authorities (including the police) with whom you have spoken in arranging for permits and other logistics. (You should keep photocopies of any permits you receive.)

4. List of speakers invited to the demonstration, time and place of their appearance, and subject matter of their remarks.

5. Logistical details: Provide names and addresses of companies or organizations supplying materials (such as sound equipment,

bullhorns, posters) for your demonstration. This section should also detail who made the original contacts, the cost of the materials, and the individuals responsible for delivering them or picking them up. Any agreements made with suppliers should be very specific. If, for example, the sound equipment does not arrive at the right place at the right time or it does not work, your demonstration can be ruined.

6. Housing: If you are expecting a large demonstration, including many people of moderate means, housing must be arranged well in advance. This section of your action plan should list all places where demonstrators can be bivouacked before and after the rally (for example, churches willing to provide temporary housing).

7. Marshals: It is always best if your group can provide its own security. Programs should be established to provide and train as many marshals as it will take to keep your demonstration from being marred by outside police action.

8. Transportation: The traditional way of transporting demonstrators from outside the Washington area to the rally is by bus. Parking for private cars is difficult to find in Washington and outrageously expensive. Buses should be chartered by your local groups (not by the central coordinating branch), but the action plan should have a complete list of all buses, their estimated time of arrival, and parking arrangements.

9. Instructions: A one- or two-page instruction sheet should be provided to all demonstrators. This will include such information as the parade route and time, rally location and speakers, housing location and cost, instructions on obeying marshals, and procedures to follow if demonstrators are arrested. It should also include the one-page fact sheet on your issue that will be described in Chapter 6.

10. Arrests and detention: Even in the best-planned and most well-intentioned demonstration, some overzealous participant is likely to be arrested. The more emotional the issue, the more likely it is that arrests will occur. This section of your action plan should outline procedures to be followed in the event that any members of your group are detained by the police. It should include names, addresses, and telephone numbers of public defenders (and other lawyers); names, addresses, and telephone numbers of responsible police officials; the name, address, and telex phone number

of the prosecuting attorney's office; and names, addresses, and telephone numbers of the individuals in your group assigned to coordinate the release of your arrested members.

The above list is not comprehensive. The logistics of even a moderate-sized demonstration are truly astonishing. Subcommittees should be convened for each of the issues listed above and a responsible individual designated to perform each of the functions. Your demonstration-coordinating committee, composed of all subcommittee chairmen, should meet frequently prior to the demonstration. If any one of the items listed above is not carefully planned in advance, your demonstration may be not only ineffectual, but downright disastrous.

Gimmicks

Gimmicks (discussed more fully in Chapter 14) are primarily designed to attract media attention. They can take almost any form; their variety is limited only by your ingenuity. If you intend to use such devices in your lobbying campaign, the action plan should contain the following:

1. description of the gimmicks to be employed

2. persons responsible within your group for planning and coordinating the gimmicks, including names, addresses, and telephone numbers of vendors as appropriate

3. permits or other licenses necessary to pull off the gimmick

4. media representatives whom you will contact for coverage of your gimmick

5. all other logistical details relating to the legality and practicality of your gimmick

As with demonstrations, most successful gimmicks are much more complicated to put into practice than they first appear. Careful planning is essential if they are to be effective.

The Hill Blitz

The Hill blitz is a traditional yet very effective method of direct lobbying. It has the advantage of involving your members in face-to-face meetings with members of Congress and Hill staff. If you have the members and time, a Hill blitz is always more effective than a demonstration. Full details on how to put together a Hill blitz are contained in Chapter 15, but for now just be sure that your action plan includes the following:

1. Names, telephone numbers, and local (Washington) addresses of all participants in the blitz.

2. Names, titles, addresses, and telephone numbers of all persons to be contacted on the Hill. (You can develop this list by following the procedures outlined in Chapter 15.)

3. Complete cross-index of dates, times of appointments, and individuals to be involved. This is the heart of the Hill blitz plan. Although it appears rather simple, developing a comprehensive appointments list is extremely time-consuming and frustrating. The master list of all appointments relevant to your individual members should be given to each. Other logistical details, including luncheons, parties, dinners, receptions, and breakfasts, should also be included in the master list.

The section of the action plan outlined above, although rudimentary, is one of the most difficult to prepare. A well-structured Hill blitz will require hundreds of telephone calls and careful supervision. The appointments section of the Hill blitz is critical. You should allocate ample time for its preparation.

Other

Depending upon the nature of your campaign, you may have a number of other sections in your action plan. These could include the following:

1. Calendars of events (congressional hearings, colloquy dates, and so on).

2. The colloquy. This section would provide names, addresses, and subject matter of congressional speakers regarding your issue, as well as persons responsible for contacting individual congressmen. (See Chapters 8 and 9.)

3. Fund-raising.

4. Expenditures: political contributions. (See Chapter 13.)

5. Resources: include contingency plans for your group and list emergency telephone numbers, names, and addresses.

If the resource book is the heart of your lobbying campaign, the action plan is the guts. The more time you spend planning, the more likely you are to succeed. Even if you ultimately decide to retain a professional lobbyist, insist that he or she provide you with an action plan. Vague promises simply do not cut ice in Washington.

Five

★ ★ ★ ★ ★

The Press

★ ★ ★ ★ ★

All politics are based on the indifference of the majority.
                                                    —James Reston

In an ideal world, perhaps laws would be made by solons deliberating the merits of issues in unbiased forums, sequestered like jurors in a murder trial from the vicissitudes of the media. In the real world, lawmakers are subjected to a barrage of outside influences, the most powerful of which is the press. Although some political theorists push the insulation theory, it simply wouldn't work in the American political system.

The influence of the press has always been a fundamental factor in American politics. The authors of the Constitution institutionalized the press as a part of the government system. Virtually nowhere else in the world is the press given the freedom and the responsibility of acting as a guardian against government excesses.

Contrary to the self-serving assertions of some journalism school professors, the media not only report the news, but also make the news. The mere appearance of a story in a major metropolitan daily can affect public opinion overnight. Media hype can make or break candidates for public office and, although Richard Nixon was undeniably paranoid about the press, the Watergate scandal probably would not have resulted in his resignation had it not been for the *Washington Post's* searing disclosures about his administration's antics. You don't have to be Nixon to hate the press or Katherine Graham to love it; as a lobbyist you must understand *how* it works.

Advertising

Anyone who has not been cloistered in a monastery for the past thirty years realizes that advertising is one of today's most powerful forces. It can induce otherwise rational people to clandestinely squeeze toilet paper in supermarkets, forsake knives for plastic contraptions that squish tomatoes, and elect proven scoundrels to high public office. As powerful as this medium is, it should be accorded the same treatment as low-yield nuclear weaponry: it is expensive and devastatingly effective when used properly, but can be either a dud or downright dangerous to the user if handled carelessly.

There are as many theories about effective advertising *means* as there are advertising *media*. Television, radio, magazines, and newspapers feverishly compete with one another to gain advertising revenues with extravagant claims about their effectiveness. The two most common mistakes political advertisers make are to believe all (or any) of the advertising media's self-advertisement and to believe they are competent to write their own copy.

Despite the popular notion that any damn fool could write better ads than those portraying mindless housewives reduced to tears over waxy yellow buildup, advertising is a highly sophisticated art. There would be plenty of room for amateurs if it were not so expensive. If your group is like most, you cannot afford to waste your money on slap-dash commercials. Full-page *Washington Post* ads do the egos of the groups placing them a lot of good, but most are so poorly written that they do not convince anybody of anything. From nine to thirteen thousand dollars per appearance, that is pretty expensive ego gratification. If you have a substantial advertising budget, you are best advised to seek professional help from an advertising agency.

One precautionary note: advertising executives are paid to produce *effective* ads, not to write erudite copy. Many groups have been dissatisfied with professional ad men because they felt the advertisements submitted were either juvenile or truncated. To an advertising person, simplicity is beautiful. You can always spot the ads in the *Washington Post* and the *New York Times* in which no advertising agency was consulted. This is particularly true in the case of foreign governments that have a penchant for publishing long diatribes by their glorious leaders. These are not read by anyone but academicians. If you pay for advertising advice, take it. You are not paying for a closely reasoned tome on the minutiae of your position; you are paying for results. You should not attempt to second-guess the professional advice you receive unless the ads submitted are grossly deceptive or scandalously mindless.

For most groups, however, their limited treasuries can best be devoted to other aspects of the media. If your position has political value, it also has media value. You can achieve more by having your position carried in news stories than through paid advertising.

How to Become Newsworthy

The first thing to understand about editors is that they tend to be conservative; that is, they would rather stick with issues that they know have a sustained, proven reader interest than to try new subjects with which they are unfamiliar. If your group or issue is relatively unknown, it is best to link your position with that of a more currently popular crusade. For example, the Flat Earth Society mentioned in Chapter 3 could link its opposition to round earth teaching in public schools to a wide variety of more traditional causes such as inflation, big government, bureaucratic waste, or parents' rights.

A corollary to the general rule that familiarity breeds ink is that what may be familiar to one editor may be Sanskrit to another. There are thousands of publications in the United States catering to virtually every conceivable interest. Your approach to editors and publishers should be multifaceted; do not gear your entire campaign to what you think will appeal to the editor of the *Washington Post*. Editors of local newspapers like a more parochial slant on issues; special interest publications need to know how your position would affect their readers. The basic rule in becoming newsworthy is to put yourself in the position of a viewer, listener, or reader of the publication you would like to publish your story. Editors respond to their constituents' needs: their job is to sell papers.

Once you determine the proclivities of a particular publication, you should not wait to be "discovered" by them. Using your resource book (see Chapter 3), call and visit the publications you have targeted. Almost all daily newspapers, radio stations, and even television broadcasters rely upon wire services or networks for their sources of news and are generally delighted to have an exclusive lead on stories of interest to their audiences. As with members of Congress and congressional staffs, reporters tend to be overworked and harassed, so the more *written* information you can provide them, the better off you will be. You will find some hard-bitten editors behind the city desk with their sleeves rolled up, but the media are businesses just like any others; a reporter's bread and butter are the sources that will give him hard stories with which to impress the boss. Don't be shy about it; prepare your facts and ask for an opportunity to speak with the powers that be.

As in all other aspects of lobbying, your relations with the press *must* be characterized by complete candor. You are playing in the big leagues, so don't attempt to be cute with your facts; it will not work. The worst thing you can do in dealing with the media is to deceive them. You may get one story with inaccurate information, but if reporters and editors believe you have intentionally misled them, you are in for a dozen adverse stories. Worse yet, stories on your issue will never grace their pages or airwaves again.

To be newsworthy over an extended period, you must retain the contacts you originally established and keep the press advised of the progress of your issue. You need not do anything particularly dramatic in this respect; merely keep your contacts informed. Follow-up stories are a good idea if you have established a rapport with some members of the press.

Talking to Reporters: Good Guys and Bad Guys

Disabuse yourself of any image you have of the infallibility of reporters or their constant dedication to the truth. Reporters are paid to write stories for newspapers; newspapers are published to make money; and news stories must be turned out at a feverish rate that does not always permit the time for background checks on the accuracy of items published or broadcast.

There is no law or even journalistic canon that requires you to treat all reporters or all publications equally. This does not mean you should declare war on any publication. Remember, the free press belongs to the person who owns one. Unless you have majority stock ownership in a newspaper chain, do not try to beat the media at their own game. Conversely, you do not have to roll over and play dead for every reporter who takes an interest in your cause. Publications do not have a constitutional right to probe your innermost thoughts on your issue; you have no obligation whatsoever to grant exclusive interviews to publications that consistently attack you. Before you make rational decisions with regard to "good guys" and "bad guys," consider the following:

1. Have you received "good press" (as defined later in this chapter) from the publication concerned?

2. Has the journalist or editor always told you the truth—that is, kept your name confidential when requested and never under those circumstances published a story in such a way that your identity was made public?

3. Despite "bad press" from the publication, would it have been possible for a *neutral* person (not you) to regard this story as fair commentary and not merely mean-spirited?

If the answer to any of these questions is no, then place that publication or reporter on your "gray" list (in politics *no one* is blacklisted—you never know when either they or you may be rehabilitated).

The gray listing of reporters or publications does not mean you will not speak to them under any circumstances; merely that they will not be favored with exclusive interviews, tips, or any off-the-record conversation. Nikita Khrushchev once said, "We will bury the West with shovels they sell us." You are not required—even by the streetfighting rules of Washington politics—to provide ammunition for the opposition. Do not, however, take the next step and attempt to exclude "hostiles" from press conferences, media events, and so on. That can only backfire on you.

If the "stick" you use against hostile press is exclusion from the inner circle, then your reward for the good guys is an understanding and sympathetic relationship. I emphasize again that the definition of good guys does *not* necessarily depend upon whether they agree with your position or consistently write sympathetic articles on your behalf. Their job is to report the news in an objective manner and to deal with you honestly. It is not only unreasonable but downright foolish to expect a reporter to write favorable stories about your group merely because occasionally she has been given exclusive interviews.

The distinction between good guys and bad guys is manifest, but it cannot be pressed too far. Even with the good guys, you should not speculate about the weaknesses in your particular issue: the reporter may feel duty-bound to report your musings and give your opponents ideas that would not have otherwise occurred to them. In short, don't be afraid to discriminate among representatives of the media, but don't start holy wars or give away the family store to your enemies.

What Is "Good Press"?

Good press certainly means more than having your name spelled right in Jack Anderson's column. It does not mean, however, that a story pointing out one or two of your warts is calamitous. In certain situations, being cast as the underdog can be an advantage.

It is easier to describe what good press is *not* than what it is. If media representation of your position does not fall into any of the following categories, you should greet it with restrained joy.

1. no press at all (your group is not mentioned; your issue is not mentioned; you are ignored)

2. "filler" stories about fringe groups (being put in the category of the "Put Pants on Dogs Movement" or the "Equal Rights for Avocados League" subjects you to such ridicule that your group may as well despair of gaining credibility with the press)

3. characterizations of your group as a bunch of fanatics or as closely allied with an extremist organization such as the Nazi party

4. accusations of illegal or immoral activities, including association with known criminals (particularly mobsters)

5. accusations that your group's stated objectives are not really your primary objective, but merely a subterfuge to accomplish other political or economic goals

6. substantiated allegations that your group is merely a "stalking horse" for other interests whose identity is secret and perhaps in conflict with your stated goals

7. substantiated allegations that your group has consciously mis-represented facts to the press and the public, has attempted to cover up unethical or immoral activity, or both

8. allegations that your group has illegally or improperly benefited from personal contact with government officials responsible for the administration of programs that you advocate

9. stories concerning internal dissension within your group, par-ticularly if such stories include references to improper conduct on the part of the leadership (such as embezzlement of money or unethical hiring practices)

There may be other types of allegations that ordinary people would cringe at, but many so-called "bad" news stories actually inure them-selves to the benefit of the organization concerned. Controversy is not necessarily bad; Ralph Nader has gained much of his strength by *remaining* controversial. It is only when the stories start to focus on subjects other than those issues you are promoting that you need to really worry. The main exception to this rule is when an apparently sympathetic story is published and it is obvious the reporter writing the story has violated established ground rules. If you made it clear that your comments were to be "off the record," and yet you were quoted by name, the reporter has committed a breach of trust that is almost unforgivable—even when he or she is on your side. A breach of confidence is simply not condoned in Washington. A reporter who would renege on his promise is a bad guy and should be dealt with accordingly.

All the above rules about determining whether a story is good or bad apply to news pieces. Opinion columns should be judged by a slightly different set of rules. Readers generally know the prejudices of the columnists and expect them to take particular positions. You should still expect columnists to observe journalistic ethics in pro-tecting sources, but these people are paid to write their opinions—*not* fact. Don't be too distressed if George Will, Mary McGrory, or Evans and Novak roast you, as long as they don't accuse you of immoral, illegal, or unethical activities. Kilpatrick's enmity may even be use-ful. As with people, groups are as well known by their enemies as by their friends. A scathing column by a well-known opponent means you have attained credibility; you may be able to use it to your own advantage. For years, Ralph Nader used to begin his speeches by saying, "As you know, General Motors doesn't like me much."

Whether and When to Say What—and to Whom

Decisions regarding statements to the press fall into two categories: when members of the press call you and when you should call them. The former situation is relatively easy to resolve. If reporters call, you should almost always speak to them, unless the caller is an absolutely unreformed bad guy. Such individuals should never be given exclusive interviews, even if just over the phone. Deal with these people only at press conferences. If a friendly or neutral reporter calls, talk to that person. Even if you don't have a story, you will have demonstrated your accessibility.

It is more likely that you will suffer from a common Washington malady: lack of press attention. In this case you will be driven to contacting the media rather than waiting for them to call you. Follow a few simple rules:

1. Be credible. Be sure of your facts and never mislead a reporter.

2. Don't call reporters until you have a real story. A generalized rendition of your position will not be of much interest to anyone unless you have a news "peg." Perhaps the most salient feature of a peg is immediacy. Don't call with information about something that took place months ago; a reporter is interested in events that either have just happened or are about to happen.

3. Do not give "exclusive" interviews to too many people. Reporters earn their daily bread by the number and credibility of their contacts. If you put out an exclusive story that *everyone* is familiar with, it is not very likely you will get the "play" you want in important publications. Worse, you will lose credibility in the eyes of those with whom you spoke.

4. Do not insist upon attribution of the story to your group. Reporters like to feel that they are independent and are (or should be) the sole judge of whether you or your group is mentioned. Your chances of being named are much better if you do not insist upon it.

5. Be sure to warn any friendly reporters you call of potential land mines in a story, which facts they might want to cross-check, and

other sources and names of your opponents so the reporters can get their views. One trick is to give reporters the name of one of your leading opponents—someone you know to be hostile to the press. You have done your duty: you have warned the reporter about the existence of opposing views and given them access to those views. If your opponent wants to put a gun to his own head, that is his own business. In doing this, be as disarming as possible. Don't attempt to state your opponent's case; merely say you don't understand his entire position but that the reporter should call Mr. X before he writes the story to get an opposing opinion.

In dealing with members of the press, one rule is immutable: never condescend to them even when they deserve it. Reporters are as dangerous as coiled cobras and will strike at the slightest suggestion of condescension. Better that you appear slightly flustered than megalomaniacal in their eyes.

The Press Release

From time to time your group should issue press releases, if only to reestablish your identity with the media. The occasions for press releases are almost infinite, but some of the most common are as follows:

1. issuance of a major policy statement

2. reaction to a statement or action by the government or your opponents

3. announcement of a press conference

4. issuance of a study prepared by your group or some other agency supporting your viewpoint

5. announcement of major media events (such as demonstrations) sponsored by your group or affiliated organizations

6. announcement of changes in the composition of your group (for example, endorsement of your group's position by other organizations)

7. announcement of major policy changes, endorsement of political candidates, or positions of other groups

Although opportunities for issuing press releases may seem endless, you should not overdo it. Few organizations have the news pegs available to justify a daily or even weekly press release. Releases should be issued only when there is a news peg to justify them. They should be, by their nature, irregular; this establishes their credibility and newsworthiness.

The press release should be written as if it were a news story you would like to see in print. Often press releases are reprinted word for word in newspapers, particularly if they are put on the wire services. You cannot blame publications for bad press if you wrote the story yourself. Be sure that all press releases are double-spaced so they are easy to read and edit, and that they contain at least the following elements:

1. date and time of release (if you wish to hold the release for a time later than the date you actually distribute it to the press, put the words *Embargoed for Release until specific date* at the top of the page)

2. a dateline (this is not just a date but the location from which the press release is issued, such as "Washington, D.C., June 6.")

3. notification, either in the letterhead of the release or typed below, that your group is responsible for preparing and issuing the release

4. the names and telephone numbers of individuals within your group from whom additional information may be obtained

Press releases should be carried by hand or faxed to the Washington offices of the publications you wish to reach. Going through the mail is an acknowledgment of the lack of immediacy of your release and substantially diminishes the chance that it will be picked up by the press. Most offices of major publications are located in the National Press Building, but you should prepare a complete address list for your action plan.

Be sure you have briefed the persons to whom you have directed further inquiries. Press releases should be carefully typed, free of errors, and cleared through a committee of your organization. No individual in your group should be given sole authority to prepare and issue releases. These are the public statements of your position. You will have to live with them for years to come. They are simply too important to be left to one person's discretion.

What If They Roast You?

You have issued your release and contacted neutral reporters and columnists, but members of the press are devastating. Half of them did not even print the story, and those who did gave you either little or blatantly hostile coverage. What do you do? There are only a few times in a lobbying campaign when humility is a virtue; this is one of them. Uniformly hostile press almost always indicates you have not done *your* job. Either your position has no merit (which, for the purpose of this book, we presume to be false) or you have made substantial errors in your media campaign. To list all the mistakes you could have made would require a separate book, but we can review the most obvious ones:

1. Your project is not newsworthy. You may have approached the wrong publications or the wrong individuals at the wrong time.

2. Your method of reaching the press did not convey a sense of immediacy and relevance.

3. You or your group lack credibility for some reason.

4. Your timing in approaching the press was wrong. Other more important news stories overwhelmed yours.

It is tempting to assume that your opponents had some influence with the press and squelched your story. Although you cannot expect your opposition to fight fair, a uniformly critical response is rarely the fault of some "bogeyman." It may seem harsh to blame only yourself, but experience will teach you that this is generally the case. However, merely because you have had one or two setbacks with the media, don't be discouraged; it's part of the Washington game. Even presidential candidates have a tough time getting good press.

Clipping Services

About the only way you will ever find out whether your stories have been carried are by having a vast network of members willing to send you copies of stories that appear in their local newspapers, going on line with a database such as Nexis, or by hiring a professional clipping service. These services review hundreds of publications every day and will send you copies of articles regarding your issue for a fixed fee plus an additional charge per clipping.

If media relations are an important part of your lobbying campaign, clipping services can serve to double-check on your effectiveness. These services will also monitor the broadcast media and send transcripts of stories carried by the networks and in some cases even local stations. Clipping services can be expensive, so content yourself with specifying merely a dozen or so publications to be reviewed. If the story has been picked up by the wire services, it will appear in virtually identical form in scores of papers. Seeing it in various publications will not do you much good; that the story made the wire services at all is most significant.

Letters to the Editor

An effective means of reaching opinion makers is through the "Letters to the Editor" column that most publications carry. Letters most often published in these columns are reactions to stories or columns previously carried by the paper or station in question. In writing letters to the editor, abide by the following rules:

1. Be brief. Letters to the editor rarely run more than one hundred words or four column inches. All publications reserve the right to edit letters for clarity and length. If your letter is too long, it will either be rejected outright or so butchered as to be unrecognizable.

2. If the writer is an officer of your group, it would be deceptive of him not to reveal that fact in the letter. Remember, your group's credibility is at stake. It can be undermined if you attempt some stunt such as submitting a letter from an apparently neutral party when in fact it is your own group's propaganda. If this is discovered by the media, you will lose more than you will gain.

3. Refer to only one issue in any letter to the editor, even if more than one subject was discussed in the article or column to which you are responding. You are unlikely to be persuasive if you are overly complex.

4. Restate the assertions in the original column or article with which you disagree. (You cannot assume that all the readers of your letter will have read the original article.) Date and sign the letter; include your address and telephone number in case the editors want to confirm that you are actually the author of the letter before they publish it.

5. Any letter to the editor that purports to state the official position of your group should be cleared with at least two other members. As with press releases, your public positions are simply too important to entrust to the judgment of a single person.

If your letter is published, be sure to distribute copies at least to members of your group.

Columnists

Columnists, despite their journalistic pretensions, are usually frustrated politicians. They don't report the news; they reduce their own prejudices to print. They are by definition not bound by the attributes of temperance and objectivity; they are *expected* to denounce various positions. They are wielders of poison pens restrained neither by fact nor good sense.

Because of their unique position within the fourth estate, you should feel free to lobby columnists just as you would congressmen or senators. Virtually the same tactics can be employed. You can plant stories with columnists much as you would insert statements in the *Congressional Record*. No columnist—and few members of Congress—will kowtow to your every request simply because you agree with her. Columnists are invariably intelligent, sensitive, and egotistical. They will not merely reprint your views any more than a member of Congress would if he disagreed with you; but when honestly and forthrightly approached, columnists welcome your assistance on a "no strings attached" basis.

A strongly worded column on your side of an issue is worth reprinting. Copies of opinion columns written by people who have no personal stake in the outcome of your campaign can be some of the most effective propaganda.

Of all the aspects of lobbying considered in this book, this chapter—the press—is the most superficially covered. Reams have been written on press relations. Since the media constitute the most powerful force outside the official government, you may be well advised to consider retaining a public relations specialist (see Chapter 17). Sometimes following the basic ground rules regarding credibility, accessibility, and common sense is just not enough to secure the press coverage you need. Public relations specialists may be an unfortunate necessity.

Six

★ ★ ★ ★ ★

Letters to the Hill

★ ★ ★ ★ ★

Politics is perhaps the only profession for which no preparation is thought necessary.

—Robert Lewis Stevenson

The primary link between members of Congress and their constituencies is the mail. Each year, millions of letters arrive on Capitol Hill. Of this blizzard of paper, only a very small portion has a discernible impact upon the course of legislative events. Most of the balance is treated as junk mail by the various congressional offices. Its receipt will be of no particular consequence to the congressman. Thus, the art of writing effective letters to members of Congress may make the difference between success and failure in your lobbying campaign.

Short and Simple: Ask for Action

A letter to a member of Congress should be addressed to her personally. There is not a single congressional office in which all mail addressed to the member automatically arrives on her desk. Invariably, mail arriving in an office will be routed through the staff. The only letters to reach the member will be those that the *staff* feels merit her attention. One of the criteria they will use in deciding whether your letter is even seen by your congresswoman is its length. Five-page, single-spaced letters almost never qualify for the member's attention. The best format is a regular business letter not exceeding two pages in length. Handwritten letters often receive special attention, particularly those with a corporation's or organization's letter-head. The letter should be brief and to the point and should always include a request for action. The following elements should be included in most letters to the Hill:

1. brief description of your organization and its objective

2. description of the issue

3. status of current law and/or pending legislation

4. effect of passage or defeat of legislation on the congressman's constituency

5. your group's position with regard to the issue

6. request for specific action on the member's part

7. reaffirmation of your group's interest in his position on this issue

A sample letter to a congressman might be as follows:

The Honorable Helen A. Toughnut
United States House of Representatives
Washington, D.C. 20515

Dear Congresswoman Toughnut:

On behalf of the members of Local 423 of the Flat Earth Society, I have been asked to inform you of a very serious issue that you will be voting on within the next few weeks. Our local is composed of 217 of your constituents, almost all of whom supported you in the last election. As you may recall, your reelection was the subject of a feature story in the *Flat Earth News*, a copy of which is attached for your consideration.

Our concern relates to H.R. 506, introduced by Congressman Undertow and currently pending in the Subcommittee on Elementary, Secondary, and Vocational Education of the Education and Labor Committee. Section 171(b) of this bill would require compulsory instruction in round earth theory in all schools receiving federal funds. There is no provision for instruction of flat earth theory.

Over the years, our group has engaged in an intensive educational program within your district on the flat earth philosophy, and we believe that a significant minority, if not a majority, of your constituents acknowledge that the earth is flat. In view of Congressman Undertow's bill, we have intensified our efforts to promote flat earthism.

We believe that Congressman Undertow's attempt to use government funds to promote his ill-conceived ideology represents an undermining of our strongly held beliefs and is a total waste of taxpayers' money.

Although we recognize that you do not sit on the subcommittee in question, we hope you will make every effort to convince the committee chairman to shelve this legislation. We are, of course, prepared to testify at any public hearings that may be held to discuss this issue. If this bill is allowed to pass, we would expect that, at the minimum, equal time be provided for instruction in flat earth theory at the elementary and secondary school levels.

For your consideration I have attached a fact sheet on the Undertow bill and a summary statement on flat earthism. Because this is a matter of some urgency, we would appreciate hearing from you soon about your feelings on this subject. Please be assured that your comments will be distributed widely here in Bedrock County. I am looking forward to hearing from you soon.

Sincerely,

Frank Bumknocker
Secretary
Flat Earth Society

In addition to the organization letter outlined above, individual members of your group should also be encouraged to write to their congressman. They should be given *only* the fact sheet mentioned in the above letter and should be encouraged to put their feelings in their own words. A sample letter should *never* be given to the members of your group.

Form Letters Are Weighed, Not Read

A clear majority of all the mail received in a congressional office consists of preprinted postcards, form letters, and handwritten letters with identical wording. Promoters of this type of approach to Capitol Hill must have incredibly low esteem for the intelligence of congressional staffers. The person charged with opening and routing mail in a congressional office needs to see only three or four identical letters before starting to put them in the "junk mail" category. The writers of such letters will get a form letter in return. It is almost a certainty that the member will never see such communications. Because form-letter campaigns are so common, the Hill has developed an extremely sophisticated method of dealing with them. The Congressional Mailing Service (CMS) is one of the best-guarded secrets of Capitol Hill. Located in the basement of a nearby office building, it is guarded twenty-four hours a day by armed Capitol police. Inside, eight million dollars' worth of electronic equipment churns out apparently "personalized" responses to incoming congressional mail.

When a form letter arrives in a congressman's office, the usual reaction of the low-level staff member is to say, "Give this guy a 44-B response." The "44-B response" is code for a form letter prepared by the congressman's staff for a particular type of letter. More sophisticated offices will even have paragraphs coded and the staffer might say, "Give these characters a 43-C first paragraph, 16-D second, and sign off with a 26-F." The more personal your letter, the less likely the congressional office will be able to adapt its form response. Because of this, you can test your congressman's responsiveness to your letters—and his attention to your issue—by analyzing his reply. If your letter identifies specific individuals, issues, and organizations, you can usually tell whether the congressman or his staffers have given it attention by noting whether his answer is directly responsive to your request. If not, it is likely you were merely fed "into the bin." The more conscientious the congressman and the more effective his staff, the less likely you are to receive a form letter.

In sum, it is a waste of money to engage in a war of computers. Your form letters will be answered by form letters, and you can be absolutely sure that the Hill's computers are better than yours. Any suggestion that your organization engage in a form-letter or postcard blizzard should almost automatically be dismissed as a waste of time and money. A well-organized letter-writing campaign, however, can be one of your most effective tools for influencing the outcome of legislation.

The Fact Sheet

The heart of an effective letter-writing campaign is apparent spontaneity. Members of your organization should write to their congressman in their own words. They should be encouraged to include personal anecdotes. Misspellings, grammatical errors, and so on are *not* important. The only things that count are that they wrote and that the facts contained in their letters are accurate.

To ensure that your members write to their congressman, it is often desirable to provide them with paper, pens, and stamped envelopes at a meeting and have them write out letters at that time. If this is logistically difficult, pleas through your newsletter to your members and telephone follow-ups are often effective. Again, the *only* written material you should provide to your members is a three- or four-page fact sheet that outlines the facts of the particular issues and your position. You should encourage your members to select one or two of the issues contained in your fact sheet and concentrate on them rather than merely rehash all of the subjects it covers. Selection of issues should be left to the individual writing the letter. This will ensure a degree of spontaneity, a quality that will be well received on Capitol Hill. Your members should be cautioned not to send a copy of the fact sheet to their congressman. This will destroy the spontaneity of the response and diminish the effectiveness of the overall campaign. The purpose of the fact sheet is to make sure that your members do not make unsubstantiated claims that could damage your group's credibility.

The fact sheet should contain the following:

1. statement of the issue
2. statement of your group's position
3. status of proposed legislation or administrative action
4. list of reasons to support (or oppose) pending legislation or administrative action
5. proposed action you wish the member of Congress to take

Unless your group's members are very sophisticated, the wording of the fact sheet should be relatively simple. If your members would

not be expected to have an intimate knowledge of congressional procedures, do not include anything in your fact sheet that would give
the impression that they have been coached. A sample fact sheet for
an average membership might read as follows:

Fact Sheet on H.R. 506:

Round Earth Amendments

Congressman Sinkum Undertow (R—NJ) has recently introduced a
bill (H.R. 506) that would amend the Comprehensive Educational
Curriculum Act of 1954. This legislation would provide for mandatory instruction in round earth theory in all elementary and secondary
schools that receive any federal funds. The bill would undermine flat
earth dogma and is a waste of taxpayers' money. The Flat Earth Society strongly opposes this legislation.

The bill is currently pending in Education and Labor Committee
in the United States House of Representatives and may come to a
vote at any time. Our Congresswoman, Helen Toughnut, has supported fairness in presenting flat earth philosophy, but it is likely that
the vote on this issue will be extremely close. The Undertow bill should
be defeated for the following reasons:

- Millions of taxpayers' dollars would be wasted in requiring teachers to undergo round earth training so that they could effectively
  promote this philosophy. This is not a legitimate government function and should at best be paid for by those groups promoting
  round earthism.

- Children are already subjected to all sorts of propaganda ranging
  from television commercials to comic books; the government should
  not subsidize additional propaganda.

- Round earth theory flies in the face of the beliefs of many patriotic
  Americans who embrace the flat earth theory and who, as parents,
  do not feel it appropriate that their beliefs be contradicted by teachers who are paid at government expense.

- Flat earth theory is accepted by scores of learned men and women
  and is at least as valid as round earth theory. It is highly discrimi-
  natory to promote one belief over another.

- The flat earth issue is fundamental. Many people will base their votes for Congressmen only on this issue.

- Round earthism is being promoted by a fringe element that does not represent the mainstream of American thought.

- Mandatory instruction in round earthism would require additional expenditure of local funds, raising the tax base for public schools at a time when inflation should be one of our primary concerns.

- The Undertow bill would create a huge federal bureaucracy, which is neither needed nor wanted by the American people.

The fact sheet should be sent with a cover letter to all of your members. They should be encouraged to write to their congressman, but *not* to include the fact sheet itself. Your cover letter should also give the complete names and addresses of Congressmen to whom you wish your members to write. The cover letter can have a somewhat more political tone than the fact sheet. A sample might be as follows:

Dear Fellow Flat Earth Supporter:

As you know, Congressman Undertow has introduced legislation that would institutionalize the teaching of round earth theory in the public schools. This legislation would be devastating to our cause and would cost millions of tax dollars. I hope you will write to your Congressmen and Senators immediately and express your opposition to the Undertow bill. For your convenience I have attached a fact sheet on this legislation. It is designed to give you some direction in preparing your letter, but your letter should be personal. *Do not* quote any of the fact sheet directly in your letter or send the fact sheet itself to the congressman. People who will have great influence on this legislation are as follows:

The Honorable Sam C. Slackman
United States Senate
Washington, D.C. 20510

The Honorable Billy K. Butterball
United States House of Representatives
Washington, D.C. 20515

The Honorable Gladys Tiltmeyer
United States House of Representatives
Washington, D.C. 20515

The Honorable Thurbridge D. Silverstein
United States Senate
Washington, D.C. 20510

    Please send us a copy of the letter you send to these Congressmen, as well as copies of any responses you receive. We will keep you posted on our progress.

Sincerely,

Melvin P. Leader

    The fact sheet and cover letter should go out as early as possible during the course of the lobbying campaign. It usually takes some time for your members to get around to writing their Congressmen. About a week after you send the letters to your members, call them to inquire whether they have written their letters. This kind of follow-up is essential for an effective grassroots campaign.

Names, Addresses, and Serial Numbers

One of the most fundamental errors made in grassroots letter-writing campaigns is to try to reach everyone on the Hill. There are 535 members of Congress; it is extremely unlikely that you will be able to have all your members write to each congressman. Depending upon the status of the legislation or administrative action, you should focus on the narrowest possible group, whether it be individual congressmen, subcommittee members, full committee members, or caucuses. If a bill has been introduced recently, it will be referred automatically to a committee and subsequently to a subcommittee. In this early stage of a bill's life, your lobbying should be directed primarily to the sub-committee members. Although there are exceptions, most sub-committees do not have a membership of more than twenty, and some have as few as five or six. You can get the names of the subcommittee members from publications such as the *Congressional Directory* and the *Congressional Yellow Book* directories published by special interest groups, or on-line via the home pages of the House and Senate. (See Chapter 19.)

The first thing to do in reviewing the subcommittee membership is to see whether you have direct constituent relationships with any of the members. It is particularly useful if any of these constituent members are inclined to be sympathetic to your position. You will need a congressional leader in any lobbying campaign; and a subcommittee member, particularly one of the majority party, can be indispensable. It is the subcommittee members who should be the first target of your letter-writing campaign. If the legislation has already been reported out of subcommittee, or if it is likely that it will be reported out despite your best efforts, your next line of offense (or defense) is the full committee. Since the full committee will have many more members, it is much more likely that you will have more direct constituent relationships with at least one or two of them. You should coordinate your campaign closely with them. Since legislation must go through an identical procedure in both the House and the Senate, you have four opportunities to focus your campaign before the issue reaches the floor. On the House side, you will have an additional opportunity. Almost all bills are routed through the Rules Committee, which acts as a traffic cop for legislation, assigning priorities for debate and establishing rules for floor consideration. This is a small but influential committee; if you have any direct constituent relationships here, you should use them.

If your issue requires the expenditure of federal funds, you will get yet another chance to present your case. Virtually all revenue measures must be considered both by the committee with jurisdiction over the subject matter (such as agriculture, banking and currency) and by the Appropriations Committee and its relevant subcommittees. The targeting procedure used with the regular committees can also be used with the Appropriations Committee.

In addition, many bills affect more than one committee's jurisdiction. For example, a bill concerning water policy might be considered by the Agriculture and the Interior committees of both the House and the Senate. Be particularly alert to this. Some of your strongest supporters may serve on one committee and be unaware that the relevant legislation is pending in another committee.

Following Up

As the coordinator of a lobbying campaign, you will have to follow up both with your own members and with the Hill. During the course of the letter-writing campaign, almost all of your group members will promise to write to their congressman, but very few actually do so. One of the best ways to tell whether your people have actually written to their congressional delegation is to *persistently* ask them to give you copies of their original letter or the response from the Hill. You will need the latter in any event to measure the effect your letter-writing campaign is having. You must actively seek the reputation of a nag if your letter-writing campaign is to be successful.

The second aspect of following up is with the Hill itself. You should get sample copies of the types of letters that individual congressional offices are sending back to your members. This will give you a good idea of where the individual members of Congress actually stand on your issue and what problems you may have. Pay particular attention to letters that suggest a general sympathy with your cause but state that the member cannot vote on your side on this particular issue. A member who indicates this position may be a prime candidate for follow-up meetings where you could discuss facts or questions about your issue.

If the response from a particular member of Congress includes facts, statistics, and so on that are simply erroneous, you should immediately draft a very polite response including the correct information and inviting the member to contact you for additional data. This draft response should be sent to the person who originally contacted the member of Congress, and that group member—not you—should forward it to the appropriate congressional office. A sample of such a letter might read as follows:

Dear Senator Belfry:

Thank you very much for your rapid response to my letter of September 5. I can certainly appreciate your position and would probably adopt it as my own if the facts were as you stated them. You noted, for example, that only federally supported elementary schools (such as schools for military dependents) would be affected by the proposed round earth bill. In fact, virtually every school in the country that receives *any* federal assistance for such programs as hot lunches would be required to comply with the round earth instruction legislation. This means, in effect, that over 95 percent of *all* schools in the United States (excluding only the rare private school that received absolutely no federal funding) would be required to comply with this federal directive. In effect, the school board here in Columbus County would not be permitted to control the curriculum of our own schools. This is a problem of immediate concern to us and not merely a philosophical consideration. This being the case, I hope you might reconsider your tentative support of this legislation and let me know how you feel.

If you need any additional information on this measure, I would be pleased to provide it for you; or, if you prefer, your staff can contact Ms. Cynthia Winetroup, our legislative representative in Washington. She can be reached at (202) 555-7416.

Thank you again for your interest and courtesy.

Sincerely,

Rebecca Moss

If a particular member persists in opposition to your cause even after you have corrected his errors, it would probably be a waste of time and energy to continue the correspondence. If the individual is critical to the passage or defeat of the legislation, it might be worth your time to pay his office a personal visit; but endless correspondence is rarely functional, particularly since the member is probably not drafting his own letters. You should find out which staffer is putting these words in the member's mouth and speak with that person directly.

If a particular member of Congress does not respond to your letters within two to three weeks, it is advisable to send her a second letter; mention the first correspondence and again request an answer. Some congressional offices are more efficient than others, and it is not unusual for smaller offices to be overwhelmed with correspondence. Some offices have even adopted a policy of responding only to letters originating within their congressional district or state. Therefore, personal visits may be required at some point.

An analysis of congressional responses may be helpful in several ways. It will enable you to get a good idea of who your supporters and opponents are. It will help you determine where your weak points are, both as a matter of votes and on the basis of which of your arguments are most consistently criticized. It may give you an idea of what kind of adjustments should be made in your lobbying campaign (based upon congressional critiques of your position, particularly if your views are misunderstood by a significant number of people). It is also a good way to detect whether your opponents have been active. The appearance of the same objections or statistics in a number of negative responses suggests that your opponents have provided the information. It is incumbent upon you to rebut them.

A letter-writing campaign can be enormously effective if it is properly administered. As with all of the aspects of lobbying, however, a letter-writing campaign involves a lot of work—not just political clout.

Seven

★ ★ ★ ★ ★

Demonstrations

★ ★ ★ ★ ★

The object of oratory alone is not truth, but persuasion.
—Lord Macaulay, *Essay on Athenian Orators*

Demonstrations or Lobbying?

Demonstrations, though sometimes necessary, are rarely the most effective or desirable means of communicating your group's views to the Congress. The chanting of slogans by faceless bodies is hardly the essence of rational debate. For example, although the massive demonstrations of the Vietnam war era had a profound impact upon government policy, the antiwar movement would have been much more effective had it devoted its considerable energy to massive lobbying rather than syncopated shouting. The U.S. withdrawal from Vietnam might have come months or even years earlier. Similarly, your members can be infinitely more effective if they walk the halls of Congress rather than the streets of Washington. One hundred lobbyists, if properly motivated and trained, can be much more effective than one thousand demonstrators.

The only circumstances in which demonstrations might be more effective than face-to-face lobbying are when you have minimal control of your group, or when supporting organizations are committed to your goals but you have no control whatsoever over their activities. In such a situation, when you don't know what your so-called supporters may do, a demonstration might be best. If you decide that a demonstration is the safest route, make sure you do it right. There are four general rules to follow if you are planning a demonstration:

1. Recognize that the demonstration is as much for the benefit of your own supporters as it is to convince the Congress or the administration of the rectitude of your views. Demonstrations can build a feeling of solidarity within your organization and encourage your members to commit themselves to your group's objectives. A Washington demonstration is a political pep rally.

2. Understand that demonstrations are media events designed to draw public attention to your issue. If you ignore this aspect of demonstrations, you may as well tell your people to stay home. The media must be carefully apprised of your plans if your demonstration is to be effective. The mere fact that you are having a demonstration or rally will not necessarily excite the press. You must also provide newsworthy events either in the form of gimmicks or well-known public speakers.

3. Since the news media are an integral part of your demonstration, you cannot allow too many of your warts to show. A noisy demonstration is one thing; an obstreperous one is another. Reporters are always alert to newsworthy events, and massive arrests are certainly newsworthy. It is rarely beneficial to encourage or even tolerate disruptive activity. You should also note that the Washington, D.C., police are so accustomed to demonstrations that it is extremely difficult to provoke them. It is highly unlikely that you will be able to characterize the Washington authorities as "fascist pigs" as credibly as you might in other cities. Thus, outright confrontation with the police is not likely to get you good press and should be avoided.

4. Demonstrations are media events, so attempt to be as visual as possible. Flags, posters, and picket signs are de rigueur in any Washington demonstration. You should not, however, encourage the display or chanting of obviously anti-American symbols or slogans. A swastika or hammer and sickle will alienate many observers who might otherwise be sympathetic to your cause.

Symbols are indeed a powerful medium, but they should be carefully chosen. The peace symbol developed in the early 1950s is a perfect example. It incorporates the semaphore "N.D."—the initials of nuclear disarmament. This symbol, though it obviously does not convey a neutral sentiment, has attained credibility far removed from radicalism.

Within the context of these general rules, successful demonstrations have a number of other hallmarks.

Invite Celebrity Speakers

In Washington almost half the population regard themselves as celebrities. Obviously this view is not universally shared outside the Washington Beltway. Since a demonstration is designed to reach many more people than just the participants, it is always a good idea to have a celebrity speaker at your rally. Be it a movie star, member of Congress, trade union official, or even a pediatrician, a "name" speaker at your demonstration will not only help attract press attention, but increase the number of demonstrators as well.

Celebrities have enormous egos, so you should brief them fully on the objectives of your demonstration as well as on who else will appear. You should also suggest issues that may not be covered by other speakers. They may not follow your precise recommendations, but you should still tell them the "party line."

In the same context, it is sometimes desirable to have entertainment provided by politically committed celebrities such as an instrumental or a singing group. These are designed more to increase the size of your demonstration than to impress the public. Often such groups will appear for free or at a greatly reduced rate. They should be approached through their agents well in advance of the proposed demonstration.

Media Relations

Much of the value of a demonstration will be lost if it does not receive adequate press coverage. You cannot expect adequate press coverage if you do not include media representatives in virtually every phase of your planning. You should issue a series of press releases prior to your demonstration detailing the logistics and objectives of your program. *Never* publicly state that one of your objectives is to achieve media attention. Obvious exploitation is a turnoff to the press. As the time for the demonstration nears, you should distribute more press releases and hold more conferences; the turnout for your demonstration depends in large measure on the amount of newsprint it has generated. The more media hype you can create, the more demonstrators you will have. The only way you will generate newsprint is through constant communication with the very people who are in turn tacitly promoting attendance at your rallies. The press should be actively included in every facet of your demonstration. The more contact you have, the more likely it is you will receive the coverage necessary to make your rally a success.

When estimating the number of demonstrators you expect, however, be conservative. The press relish demonstrations at which only a fraction of the predicted number turn out, but also love to report demonstrations that exceeded the planner's initial projections.

Signs and Symbols

As noted previously, symbols are an extremely effective method of political communication. They can convey a philosophy far more quickly than can rhetoric. If possible, your group should design its own symbol, one that will evoke sympathy or at least understanding. You should, however, avoid incorporation of existing radical symbols into yours. Raised fists, burning crosses, fasces, swastikas, and red stars leave the majority of Americans with a negative impression. You do not want to alienate potential allies by using emotional signs or symbols; rather, you want to develop an identity of your own.

Once you have adopted a symbol, it will become known only if it is frequently and obviously used. It should be displayed prominently at all rallies and demonstrations and carried on picket signs, T-shirts, and any other promotional piece you use. The National Farm Workers' eagle is an example of a brilliantly conceived and executed symbol, recognizable by millions of Americans. It is a statement by itself and makes no reference to other political ideologies.

Timing

Good weather for a demonstration is often critical. Few but the absolutely committed will march down Pennsylvania Avenue in a thunderstorm. Luckily, weather in Washington is very predictable.

Winters are gray and moist; temperatures rarely fall below 25° Fahrenheit. Spring (late March to mid-May) is beautiful, with temperatures in the mid-70s most of the time; but there are frequent showers. Summers (through mid-September) are very hot and humid. Autumn is the best time of year; the evenings are cool, and there is low humidity and easily predictable rain. All other factors being equal, a demonstration held in late September or early October would offer the best possibility of a good turnout. If you must hold a demonstration at another time of the year and are expecting many participants from outside the Washington area, be sure to warn them about the Washington climate and advise them to dress appropriately.

In planning your demonstration you should also be sensitive to the schedule of the Congress. A rally in August will rarely attract much congressional attention; all the members of Congress are back in their home districts mending political fences. In election years, the Congress breaks for the Republican and Democratic conventions and takes an extended leave of absence for the campaign. Other traditional congressional holidays include Memorial Day, Independence Day, Labor Day (usually a week), Thanksgiving (three days), Christmas (a week or so), President's Day, Easter, Martin Luther King's Birthday, Jefferson's Birthday (a largely Democratic holiday given to fundraising speeches), and any time there is more than a foot of snow on the ground. Since the President generally tries to work his absences from Washington around the congressional calendar, you should look to both the legislative and administrative branches' schedules in timing your demonstration. This information is available on the Internet home pages of the House (http://www.house.gov) and Senate (http://www.senate.gov).

Also vital to the timing of your demonstration is the relative availability of your members. Many organizations rely upon young people to fill out their demonstrations. If this is the case with your group, demonstrations during Thanksgiving and spring college breaks are a good idea. For family-oriented issues, weekends when working parents are available are best. Warmer months are preferred for campaigns directed to the needs of the elderly.

Aside from manpower considerations, your demonstration should be timed to coincide with a major breakpoint in public policy. Such breakpoints can include:

1. a vote on the Senate or House floor on legislation affecting your issue

2. a previously announced decision date by the Administration on an issue affecting your group (this includes agency as well as White House deadlines)

3. anniversary dates commemorating events significant to your organization

Momentum, a factor that is admittedly much vaguer than the types of dates listed above, is also an important factor in the timing of demonstrations. When public interest in your campaign is on the rise, a demonstration can serve both to maintain it and fuel its fires.

Appeal to Justice

Many demonstrators believe they can achieve their objectives through the shock value of silly, iconoclastic charades. Although such antics may make the evening news, they rarely impress policy makers. Your demonstration is more likely to stir up sympathy if it stresses the fundamental justice of your cause. People react more favorably to perceived injustices than to insults. Thus you should focus your demonstration on your objections to being treated unfairly. A good example of this is the proabortion movement. This group characterizes itself as the "Freedom of Choice Movement" rather than as proabortion.

Avoid Zealotry

During the course of any lobbying campaign and particularly during demonstrations, there is always a temptation to be carried away by the mood of the moment. Emotionalism is fine, but it cannot be allowed to override common sense. Intemperate comments can harm your campaign if they don't really convey what you mean. This is not to suggest that strident words do not have a place in a demonstration; they do. A dispassionate demonstration is not very exciting to watch. There is a narrow line, however, between justified emotion and mindless fanaticism. A good partisan speech can be turned, with little effort, into the frantic ramblings of a zealot. There is no guide to help you distinguish between the two other than common sense.

You can, however, do something about the fanatics in your own camp. If you know in advance that some demonstrators are extremist, you can keep them segregated from the rest of your troops. (For example, in the later demonstrations of the antiwar movement, those committed to the cause of North Vietnam were carefully isolated from the more moderate.) Under no circumstances should you permit extremists to share the podium with rational adherents to your cause. Reporters are delighted by uninhibited rhetoric; and your entire campaign, no matter how defensible, may rise or fall on the ravings of these fringe elements.

Dealing with the Police

In large demonstrations, no matter how careful your planning, you will have to deal with the police. In Washington this sometimes means coordinating your activities with at least four different police forces. Washington has, at last count, fourteen different constabularies. The four most prominent police agencies with which you will have to deal are the Metropolitan Police Department (MPD), the Capitol Police, the Park Police, and the Executive Protective Service (the uniformed branch of the Secret Service). As noted previously, Washington police forces have extensive experience in dealing with demonstrations and are unlikely to be provoked except in the most extreme circumstances. Despite popular mythology, the Washington police agencies are generally professional and cooperative, and they sometimes even have a sense of humor. Many groups have come to Washington expecting—even hoping for—confrontations, only to be disappointed by the courtesy of the cops. All four agencies noted above have community relations departments designed to assist you in planning and carrying out your demonstration. The departments will not only help you establish parade routes, but provide police protection rather than harassment. They will help you train your marshals and will cooperate with them during the demonstration itself. In short, you cannot afford not to cooperate with the police. They can suppress violent opposition, make your demonstration orderly, clear streets for your group, and even make sure such necessities as toilet facilities are available. If you plan to have a demonstration, do not fail to contact the police well in advance.

Community Relations

Washington has endured so many demonstrations that the reactions of its residents are almost unique: they don't take them too seriously. They tend to regard them as one of the hazards of living in the nation's capital. This attitude changes, however, if the demonstration either generates substantial inconvenience or is a conscious attempt to promote goodwill in the city.

A perfect example of this occurred a few years ago. At one point, farmers from the American Agriculture Movement were almost literally run out of town for driving their tractors up and down the Mall, destroying the shrubbery and buckling the sidewalks. A short time later they were greeted as saviors for bringing those same tractors to snowbound streets and rescuing stranded motorists. Neither action had much to do with their issue, but they left with more goodwill than when they entered. Remember, many Washingtonians are lobbyists, congressional staff members, and bureaucrats. If your group can attract their attention in a positive way—even if it has nothing to do with your policy objectives—you are well ahead of the game.

Washington is a city with all the ills of most urban areas and, as such, has an enormous potential for community relations projects. Virtually any such project your group undertakes will get attention, which, cannot help but benefit your organization. For example, if your group advocates clean water, a symbolic cleanup of the Potomac River would ensure not only good press, but community sympathy. A visit to a local abortion clinic might engender good press for both proabortion and antiabortion groups. The possibilities are endless. Even if the community relations project is only tangentially related to your primary issue, the good public relations your group receives will be noted by the people on the Hill who matter. One hundred demonstrators cleaning up an inner-city alley will receive as much coverage as the same number of demonstrators getting arrested. It may seem callous to suggest that community projects should be done for the purpose of public relations, but it is shocking that more groups do not recognize the value of this tactic.

Logistics

It is easy enough to announce a demonstration in Washington; it is something else to actually have one. There are hundreds of details with which you must concern yourself. A few of them follow.

Permits

If you plan even a small demonstration, you must secure permits from the city as well as the federal government. For information regarding required permits, contact the police agencies noted above.

Housing

Washington has one of the highest ratios of hotel rooms to resident population of any city in the country. Nevertheless, adequate housing is always at a premium, particularly during the spring and summer. You should be sure all demonstrators have shelter during their stay in Washington. If hotel space is unavailable or is too expensive for your group, there are numerous agencies (such as churches) that may be able to assist you. Camping out is *not* a viable option in the immediate vicinity of Washington, so appropriate lodging is a necessity.

Transportation

Buses are the traditional method of bringing demonstrators to Washington. Within the city there is an excellent system of transportation. Buses regularly stop in all parts of the city, and a subway—the Metro—provides rapid access to Capitol Hill and the downtown area. You may want to consider bivouacking your demonstrators at the terminus of the subway lines, where housing rates are cheaper.

Miscellaneous

To be effective, a demonstration must have adequate posters, sound systems, sanitary facilities, food, and other necessities. Although such accommodations may seem obvious, you would be surprised at how many demonstration organizers forget that people need to eat—the result being demonstrators scattered over a twenty-block area searching for hot dogs when they should be at a rally. You must pay as much attention to the needs of your demonstrators as you do to the specifics of your issue. In large demonstrations, it is imperative that you provide first-aid services. Invariably, a number of demonstrators will be injured, suffer from heat prostration, or suffer more severe maladies.

You should also be alert to various fund-raising possibilities: selling food to hungry demonstrators; selling buttons, banners, T-shirts, and other paraphernalia related to your cause. If this sounds mercenary, remember, both Pat Robertson and Abbie Hoffman advocated the same tactics. A demonstration is a kind of carnival; there is no political or moral rule that prohibits you from gaining additional funds to promote your position.

Eight

★ ★ ★ ★ ★

The Congressional Hearing

★ ★ ★ ★ ★

Laws are like cobwebs which catch many small flies, but let wasps and hornets break through.

—Jonathan Swift

One of the ways to get exposure for your group is to testify at congressional hearings. These hearings are held by Senate and House committees and subcommittees and are almost always open to the public. As such, they are extensively covered by the press and provide a good vehicle for increasing your public recognition.

What Are Congressional Hearings?

Congressional hearings are an essential part of the legislative process. Although some legislation is adopted without full subcommittee hearings, that is the exception. After a bill is introduced, it is referred to a standing committee; the chairman of that committee then refers the bill to one of the subcommittees within his or her jurisdiction. The subcommittee chairman, in turn, will schedule hearings on the matter. Such scheduling is a matter of discretion. If hearings are not put on the calendar of the subcommittee, it is unlikely that the legislation will pass. (There are ways to have a bill reported out of the full committee without hearings, but this is a rarely used parliamentary maneuver.)

Congressional hearings are of two basic types: legislative hearings and oversight hearings. Legislative hearings are by far the most common. They are held to consider bills that have been introduced by members of Congress and referred to the committee or subcommittee concerned with the general issue. Often a committee will consider a series of bills related to a single subject at one hearing. Legislative hearings are usually announced well in advance, and the chairman of the committee or subcommittee will request the views of the administration as well as those of interested parties. These hearings may last from a few hours to several days, as in the case of appropriations bills.

Oversight hearings, on the other hand, are generally held to review the effectiveness of *existing* legislation. They are usually called when there is some obvious problem with the administration or enforcement of the statute. In broad terms, the Watergate hearings and investigations of malfeasance by the administrative branch can be characterized as oversight hearings. Although they may well be more important, the time spent on congressional oversight is far exceeded by that devoted to new legislation. Oversight hearings tend to focus first on the executive branch; often the General Accounting Office is called to testify regarding their investigation of the agency charged with malfeasance or nonfeasance. The agency or department being investigated is almost always called to defend its record, and there is usually an opportunity for the public at large to present its views. During the course of oversight hearings, new legislation may be introduced to correct the apparent deficiencies.

Although there is a practical difference between oversight and legislative hearings, this distinction is not raised to the level of law or parliamentary procedure as far as members of Congress are concerned. To them, a hearing is a hearing; any matter relevant to the general subject matter under consideration may be taken up. It is not unheard of for new legislation to actually be drafted in the middle of an oversight hearing.

How to Have a Congressional Hearing Scheduled

As noted previously, the scheduling of a congressional hearing is decided on by the chairman of the committee or subcommittee concerned. Since very few legislative measures are enacted into law without hearings, scheduling is critically important. During any legislative session, fewer than one-third of the bills introduced ever receive consideration in hearings. If all bills received the attention of a full-scale hearing, Congress would either have to double its membership or be involved in committee action 24 hours a day, 365 days a year.

Often a number of bills will be considered in the same hearing, but only one or two will actually receive serious attention. The balance will be shunted aside or ignored. It is, therefore, critically important to any measure you are supporting that thorough hearings on it be scheduled early in the legislative session. Hearings held just prior to adjournment, particularly during election years, are likely to lead nowhere; there will be no time to adequately consider the proposals on the floor, even if they are affirmatively reported out of committee. Conversely, if you are opposing a particular legislative initiative, one of the easiest ways to kill it is by delaying active committee consideration.

With notable exceptions, few bills are passed that are not accompanied by a committee report. If you support a bill, your opponents' first tactic will be to delay consideration of your measure in committee. Therefore, your first obligation must be to secure early hearings. This, like much of the art of lobbying, is not as simple as it first appears. Unless your measure is cosponsored by the committee chairman or is an "administration bill" submitted by the president or the executive branch, hearings are not automatic. As previously noted, the scheduling of such hearings is entirely up to the discretion of the committee chairman. That person must be convinced that there is considerable congressional interest in your measure and, preferably, she should agree with your objectives.

While it is not essential that the chairman be one of your allies, his active opposition severely reduces your chances of success. This person knows that failure to hold hearings can wreck most legislation. It is, therefore, advisable to approach the chairman early in the game, preferably shortly after the legislation has been introduced. This should be done by the same method as other staff contacts (see Chapter 11). You should also ask your other congressional supporters to contact the chairman requesting hearings. Sometimes direct congressional influence that you could not achieve independently can be brought to bear. If you encounter intractable resistance from the committee chairman, you should consult your other congressional allies and determine whether the measure might be considered in another committee or could be reported out of committee by parliamentary maneuvering, which has been successfully employed with many controversial measures. Going over the chairman's head, although unusual, may be your only hope in certain circumstances. Even when the chairman is not overtly hostile, however, hearing schedules often slip. While observing congressional etiquette, you must be constantly vigilant to the institutional procrastination of the Hill.

How to Be Invited to Testify at a Congressional Hearing

Outside Washington, testimony at congressional hearings conjures up images of klieg lights, television cameras, and instant fame. Although that is sometimes the case, it is highly unlikely that you would want such hoopla at your hearing. The press, particularly the broadcast media, covers congressional hearings thoroughly only when the scent of scandal is in the air. The most widely covered congressional hearings are oversight rather than legislative hearings. To get CBS network news involved, there must have been a massive foul-up somewhere. So, unless you are an expert in media manipulation such as Ralph Nader, don't try to make your name in an oversight hearing. Stick to legislative hearings your first time out.

Most congressional hearings are pretty tame by Hollywood standards, and it is not difficult to be invited to testify if you play your cards right. Once you have been successful in getting a hearing date, be sure to talk to the staff members who serve both your congressional allies and the committee. You should make it clear to them that you are anxious to testify at the hearings and that you are prepared to keep your testimony short. As an added inducement, it is sometimes a good idea to hint that a well-known spokesman of your cause will be the person who actually testifies. This is particularly useful if the spokesman is an important constituent of members on the committee.

Although it is not always the case, such celebrity spokesmen will not always be as well briefed as their Washington representatives (or you). If the price of being permitted to testify is to have your celebrity do the talking, there are a number of practical rules to follow. *Never* allow such people to speak extemporaneously before a congressional committee. If they are well known enough to impress the Hill, their remarks will probably also be picked up by the press. Sometimes celebrity advocates can undo weeks of work with a few simple, stupid statements. They can undermine carefully refined positions if they are unfamiliar with the facts and your efforts. Worst of all, if their testimony departs in any significant respect from the information you have already given the Hill, your entire group's credibility can be damaged or destroyed. If you bring in one or more uninformed celebrities to testify, be sure to write their testimony, and don't let them depart from it. You should also personally accompany them to the witness table and be prepared to kick them in the shins if they start ad-libbing. Celebrity witnesses are an excellent way to be sure your group is permitted to testify, but they cause extreme embarrassment if they are not fully apprised of the facts and your position.

In addition to orally requesting an opportunity to testify, you should also send a formal request to the committee and subcommittee chairmen, observing any deadline date specified by the committee itself.

The Statement

In almost all congressional hearings, you will have two opportunities to present your views: an extensive written statement and live testimony. Both will be included in the record. It is never a good idea to merely prepare a four- to five-page speech and read it at a congressional hearing. This is condescending and insulting, particularly since most committees require you to submit twenty copies of your comments in advance. If you insist on it, though, be prepared to catch glimpses of committee members reading other material, checking the latest stock market quotations, or reading Doonsbury while you testify.

In preparing testimony, your written statement should contain a detailed analysis of your position. Depending on the issue, it can be twenty or more pages long (but never more than thirty). This is basically a staff document; in unusual circumstances it can provide backup for a congressman who becomes actively interested in your subject. It can include graphs, charts, and other data that would be difficult to read into the record.

Your oral statement, on the other hand, should *not* be distributed to the committee prior to the hearing. In fact, it should not be typed at all. Your oral statement should consist primarily of notes or a typed summary of the most important points you want to make. It should contain numerous references to your written statement, but it should not attempt to incorporate all the points you have made in writing. Your oral testimony should be dramatic. You want to have the committee's attention, but you will not get it if you merely repeat what you have already written in your prepared statement. Despite all the dictates of common sense, most witnesses at congressional hearings insist upon reading the driest sort of nonsense from a prepared script.

Congressional hearings are part solemn legislative sessions, part carnival, part high drama, and part transparent charade. Remember, however, that in order to be truly effective, the presentation of your case before a congressional committee demands accuracy, forcefulness, and spontaneity.

Most committees require the prepared statement be submitted two to three days in advance of the actual hearing. You should carefully check the specific requirements of the relevant committee to determine the number of copies required and try to meet the deadline. Your written statement should be very carefully proofed. Since all witnesses must submit their statements at the same time, you may be able to get a sneak preview of what your opposition will be saying prior to the hearing if you have developed your staff contacts well. Many people, including the press, will have the same idea, and staffs are usually reluctant to part with advance copies of statements.

On the day of the hearing, you should bring another twenty-five to thirty copies of your written statement. There will almost always be a press table where other witnesses, members of the press, and spectators can pick up copies. Although the original filing with the committee is supposed to take care of such needs, it almost never does. If you expect to be given adequate exposure by the media, this should be considered more than a mere courtesy. Most stories are prepared from the written statement and not the oral testimony at hearings.

If you have secured advance copies of other witnesses' testimony, do not make a public issue of that fact. You have gained an advantage (by being able to take into account your opposition's as well as your allies' arguments when preparing your own testimony), but gloat only in private. If you do so publicly, you will not receive the same favor again. Even if you are unable to get advance copies of all testimony prior to the hearings, you should at least be able to secure the statements of those organizations sympathetic to your cause. Duplicate statements by several groups on the same issue rarely accomplish much; your appearance will be much more effective if you have a coordinated presentation.

Often the committee will call panels of witnesses rather than individual witnesses. This is particularly the case when several witnesses share the same general perspective on the issue. Unless specifically requested to do so by the subcommittee chairman or staff, however, you should not volunteer to appear as a panel member in lieu of testifying individually. The impact of your individual statement will be diluted if there are five other people at the witness table while you are testifying.

In most congressional hearings, witnesses are seated at a table facing a horseshoe–shaped dais. The members sit at the dais with the staffers behind them. Try to maintain eye contact throughout your statement, referring to your notes only briefly. You should be accompanied by at least one assistant who can arrange supplemental information and give it to you quickly if you are asked questions. You shouldn't have to fumble with papers when you are trying to be responsive.

Planting Questions

It may not seem proper that questions are actually planted with congressmen before a congressional hearing, but if you are to be an effective Washington lobbyist, you will have to get over your queasiness and play the game by Washington rules. Few congressional staffs and even fewer members of Congress have the opportunity to fully research your issue before the hearing. They are unlikely to know the strong and weak points of your arguments or those of your opposition. Judicious questioning can bring these out. Planting questions should not be considered a trick you play on your opponents. Leading questions can be one of the best ways for you to emphasize critical points, even when you have already discussed the issue in your primary testimony (known as testimony in chief). Conversely, a direct question from a congressman on an issue for which your opposition is ill prepared can be more devastating than a direct attack in your own testimony.

If you decide to plant questions, be sure to clear them with the staff of the committee as well as with the personal staff of the member posing the question. Generally the staffs will agree to have the member ask your question if it appears fair and reasonable. The most important thing about planting questions, however, is that you must also supply the *answer* to any query you plant. This is especially important for questions to your opposition. The member of congress posing the question must be able to follow up her line of examination with a second or third query if the initial answer she receives is not satisfactory. She won't be able to do this unless she has been fully briefed. She must be given not only the answer you anticipate your opposition will give, but also factual information regarding *your* point of view. Planted questions can easily backfire unless your questioner is both adroit and knowledgeable.

Be sure the questions you plant that are to be directed to you are not "softballs." A rhetorical question such as "Isn't it true, Mr. Witness, that if your position is not adopted it will cost the taxpayer forty-five billion dollars for no appreciable benefit?" won't win you any points. Such questions are so transparently biased that your answer will convince no one. Your planted questions must preserve the semblance of neutrality even though you are obviously an advocate for a particular point of view. You cannot draw the congressman publicly too far onto your side of the issue if he is to maintain his effectiveness as an arbiter.

Answering Questions

Answering questions in a congressional hearing is a finely developed art. Unlike in a courtroom trial, witnesses are not required or even expected to respond merely "yes" or "no" to questions. Although you are not necessarily entitled, as a matter of law, to an attorney at a congressional hearing, if you choose to have one he can sit right next to you and coach you on your answers.

Unlike judges, congressmen are not neutral triers of fact. They are strongly biased and often exhibit their personal prejudices. This being the case, your answers to congressional questions should fit the circumstances. You should be as aggressive in answering questions as your questioner is in posing them. Do not be intimidated by hostile questions. Politely but firmly insist that you be permitted to give a complete answer to complex questions, and don't allow yourself to be bullied into answering "yes" or "no" to questions that have no simple response. Conversely, do not provide more information than the questions call for. If, for example, the president of the Flat Earth Society were asked whether his organization received any corporate contributions, he might answer, "Yes, approximately five percent of our total operating budget is provided by foundations that are in turn funded by corporations. We do not now or have we ever accepted any direction or control from corporations." A mere affirmative answer to the question could leave the impression that the organization was somehow a toady to big business.

Try to answer friendly questions with a straight face even when they are obvious softballs. One trick is to make the question appear to be more complex than it really is. For example, in responding to the question about taxpayers' cost of $45 billion, the Flat Earth Society president might respond that the $45 billion is a maximum estimate spread over a five-year period, but that the first-year costs would exceed $13 billion. In general, avoid demagoguery, and attempt to make even your friendly questioner appear to be a model of propriety.

If more than one member of your group is sharing the witness table with you, it is sometimes a good idea to permit others to answer one or two of the questions, particularly if the query falls in their area of expertise. Often, a different perspective on a given question is useful; even different phraseology used by your associates may provide a useful insight.

If you are asked questions for which you have no ready answer or that will require additional research, say so immediately: don't attempt to bluff. You are dealing with experts in the art, so don't attempt to con them. In the event that you cannot answer a question and offer to provide additional information at a later date, be sure to do so as soon as possible. Such additional information should be supplied in writing to the committee staff, the committee chairman, the member who asked the question, and all other members of the committee who attended the hearing. If possible, such answers should be provided within forty-eight hours following the hearing so that the issue is still fresh in their minds.

During the course of a hearing, other witnesses will also be asked questions, some of which you will wish *you* had been asked. If such questions are asked before you testify, don't be reluctant to answer them yourself in person, even if you are not asked them (put them in your testimony in chief). If the questions occur after you testify, respond to them in writing (again within forty-eight hours) to the committee staff, the committee chairman and all other members who attended the hearing. In such follow-up answers, be sure to request that your response be included in the formal record.

Press Coverage

The press can be expected to cover relatively few congressional hearings. Every day there are literally scores of committee and subcommittee hearings on every imaginable issue. Your hearing, although it may seem phenomenally important to you, may be less than impressive to callous national editors of major newspapers. Difficult as this may be for you to accept, it is *your* obligation to make your issue newsworthy; you cannot merely blame the press for political myopia.

Every time you testify before a congressional committee, your organization should issue a press release. The release should summarize the testimony of your witness and should not exceed two pages. It should be in the form specified in Chapter 5 and marked "Embargoed For Release Until [date and time of your testimony]." The press release should be distributed at least twelve hours before you are due to testify. If you wait until the actual testimony is given, you will often miss deadlines and get no coverage at all. You should also agree to make yourself available for questions by the press immediately following your testimony. Part of the value of testifying before a congressional committee is the coverage you will receive. You should maximize it.

The Record

During the congressional hearing, constant reference is made to the "record." Although this sounds extremely official, it is much less precise than you might imagine. In most congressional hearings, there is a professional stenographer who transcribes the testimony of all witnesses. Don't take this too seriously. If you muff it, you will have an opportunity to correct the record by judiciously editing those portions of the hearing transcript in which you spoke. Before the hearing starts, be sure to speak with the stenographer and ask for a copy of the draft transcript. You should also check with the secretary of the committee to be sure you will have an opportunity to correct your remarks. A week or so after the hearing, you will receive a rough draft of the transcript if you have requested it. Invariably, you will hardly recognize what you said. The stenographer includes all the fumbles of your speech—all the "and uhs," "you knows," and so on. Make changes as appropriate and return your corrections to the committee. Be sure to keep a copy of the corrected transcript for yourself. It is not unknown for a transcript to be lost in the mail.

At the hearing you will pick up copies of statements of all other witnesses if you have not already done so. If your relations with the committee staff are good, you can also get unedited copies of the entire transcript including your opposition's statements. If the committee staff is less than cooperative, you can sometimes get full transcripts from the reporting service that hired the stenographer. The Hill still contracts for stenographic assistance and rarely uses its own people. If you do go to the independent reporting service to get a complete copy of the transcript, be sure to inquire about the per-page cost. Some transcription services charge up to $2.50 a page for advance copies.

After you get a corrected copy of the record of the hearing—which is usually published two to three months after the hearing—be sure to send it to all your supporters. It is also useful to submit your statement to be printed in the *Congressional Record* very shortly after the hearing itself. This is a transcript of floor proceedings but also includes other partisan political speeches. Your statement will appear here within four to five days. This assures wider readership of your position and is good public relations. It can be done by working through the personal staff of a congressman (see Chapter 9).

The congressional hearing is one of the best opportunities for you to lay out your public position with a maximum of media coverage. Although few hearings are as thoroughly covered as those seen on the network news, they are an indispensable part of the legislative process and should be exploited to your fullest advantage.

Nine

★ ★ ★ ★ ★

The Congressional Record

★ ★ ★ ★ ★

If they put Congress' collective brain in a grasshopper, it would hop backwards.

—McEonald J. Beavers

What Is the *Congressional Record*?

If you believe the claims of some congressmen, the *Congressional Record* is the repository of all political wisdom. It is cited as the authority for wildly varying claims and is footnoted in innumerable speeches, books, articles, and even learned journals. In reality, 80 percent of the information that appears in the *Congressional Record* can be cited only for the fact that it appears in the *Congressional Record*.

The *Congressional Record*, in addition to being the minutes of legislative sessions, also includes hundreds of pages of partisan political speeches delivered by members, as well as additional data, speeches, articles, charts, government studies, poetry, newspaper editorials, and recipes for corn bread. Until a few years ago, it was impossible to distinguish between what a congressman had actually said on the floor of the Senate or the House and what he merely "tossed in the hoppers." (The "hopper" is a basket located on the clerk's desk in the

Senate or House chamber. Inserts for the *Congressional Record* are placed in it by a member, and these are then collected by the Clerk and passed on to the Government Printing Office.) Now if a congressman did not actually say the words that are printed, a discreet bullet precedes the printed version. The *Congressional Record* could never survive a truth-in-advertising investigation under the same standards applied to most commercial products.

Nevertheless, the *Congressional Record* is an indispensable tool for the lobbyist. The last dozen or so pages of the daily *Record* contain a relatively complete agenda of bills introduced, committee meetings scheduled, and record votes, along with cursory status of legislation. And no lobbyist can be without the roll-call vote listings on important legislation. Sometimes even the debates are worth reading; certainly the members of Congress would like you to believe they are. They spend millions of dollars every year reprinting speeches that appeared in the *Record* and sending them to their constituents.

How to Be Included in the *Congressional Record*

Although the quality of debate in the *Congressional Record* may not meet nineteenth-century British parliamentary standards, it is still useful to have your views published there. In the first place, it's free. Second, reprints of a *Congressional Record* statement make impressive propaganda pieces for your supporters. Third, many Hill staffers read the *Record*, and you may as well reach this audience.

One of your easiest tasks as a lobbyist will be getting your views reprinted in the *Record*. You need only prepare the documents to be inserted, check their accuracy, and give them to a member of Congress who is willing to toss them in the hopper. *Congressional Record* insertions can include newspaper editorials favorable to your position, speeches given by proponents of your views, articles on your issue that have appeared in other publications, statements made before congressional hearings, and even specially prepared statements by the congressmen themselves.

You should always attempt to have the statements you've made before congressional hearings included in the *Record* (see Chapter 8). In preparing the insertions, draft a two-paragraph introduction that incorporates the congressman's endorsement of the documents to be inserted. You should deal principally with his staff in requesting insertions in the *Record*. You should also be extremely careful about the accuracy of these requested insertions. If comments placed in the

Record are inaccurate or scandalous, the member may be somewhat embarrassed, but your reputation will be severely damaged. The marginal gains achieved by having information printed in the *Record* are outweighed by the harm erroneous material can cause.

Reprinting of Remarks

After an item has appeared in the *Congressional Record*, many members will have that portion of the publication reprinted as a one- or two-page flier for distribution to constituents. Congressional reprints can be used for general information purposes, as campaign propaganda, in research, and for other nonlegislative activities.

Each congressional office has its own method of handling the enormous cost of reprinting items from the *Record*. If the member chooses to reprint an item, you may be able to help her and your own cause by absorbing part of the expense of mailing it to your membership. You should, however, be extremely sensitive to the legal and political implications of any suggestion that you provide financial assistance. If necessary, the staff can request a ruling from the Ethics Committee regarding this issue.

If you cannot convince the congressman to distribute the reprinted *Record* item at his own expense, you may still be able to get additional copies for your group at very low cost. Consult with the congressional office about using government printing services for this purpose.

Ten

The Staff

A politician is a person with whose politics you don't agree; if you agree with him, he is a statesman.

—David Lloyd George

Who Are They? What Motivates Them?

At last count, congressional staff members numbered more than seventy-five hundred—not counting the thousands in support positions such as policemen, doormen, and so on. Staffers are the backbone of the Hill. No legislation is defeated or passed without their agreement or at least acquiescence. They are, in effect, the fourth branch of government.

Given their enormous power, they obviously play an important role in any lobbying campaign. As often as not they are ignored by inexperienced lobbyists (who, as often as not, lose).

Many people believe that their message won't get through unless they see "the member." This is almost always false. If a lobbyist ignores the staff, a meeting with a member of Congress will be for the sake of appearances only. The congressman will generally exude sympathy for the lobbyist's cause and mutter vague promises about future action. The moment the lobbyist leaves the room, the congressman will call in his staffer and demand to know what the prior conversation was all about. If the staff member has not been thoroughly briefed by the lobbyist, she will almost certainly scuttle any request the lobbyist has made to the congressman.

Keep in mind that congressional staffs are influenced by a variety of job demands and factors.

Protecting the Congressman

Staff members' first obligation is to protect their boss. They will be extremely cautious about advising the member to take positions that could stir controversy and expose him to criticism. They are also responsible for seeing that he is well briefed *before* he states a position so he doesn't make a fool of himself in public.

Promoting the Congressman

One of the primary roles of staffers is to get their boss reelected. Their jobs depend upon it. Constituent problems are thus a top priority for most congressional offices. If you can convince the staff that your position will promote the congressman's chance of reelection, you are already halfway home.

Researching and Briefing

Every year, more than twenty thousand separate bills are introduced in the Congress; that's more than five hundred thousand pages of proposed legislation. Neither congressmen nor their staffs can hope to even read the bills themselves, much less understand the fine points of the potential laws. It's not that staff members are lazy; the deluge of paper simply overwhelms them. As a lobbyist, your job is to do the staffers' work for them. Staffers can call upon the Congressional Research Service (CRS), a branch of the Library of Congress, to prepare "briefing papers," but these papers are almost always neutral. They state facts—not political reasons. Staff members are uniformly grateful for short, straightforward, accurate, and honest briefing papers (see "The Summary Sheet" in Chapter 11).

Ego

Overworked, harassed, and often ignored, congressional staff members still know they are an essential part of the legislative process. It is an anomaly of American politics that a vast majority of Hill staffers

Personal Staff of a Congressman or Senator

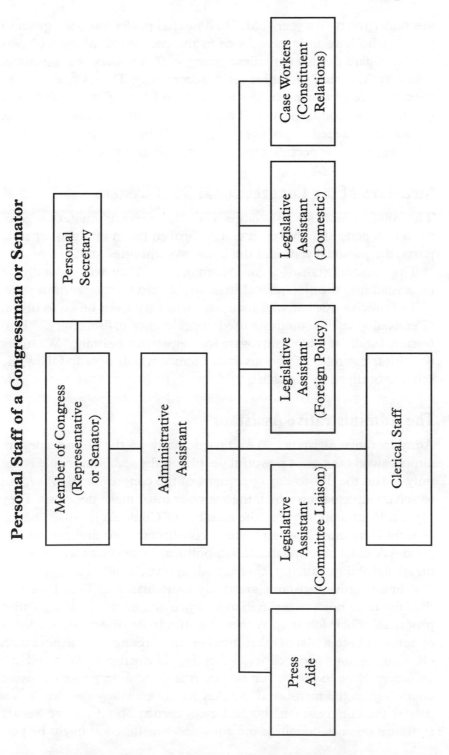

are under thirty-five years old. Phenomenal power has been given to people who have little experience in the real world. Many lobbyists tend to regard dealing with these young staff members as a distasteful necessity. The staff members react accordingly. They *know* they are inexperienced in many of the areas in which they must work, but deeply resent condescension. These are intelligent, sensitive people. Although hardened by politics and generally immune to outright flattery, they want respect. A good lobbyist will give it to them.

Structure of the Congressional Staff System

The congressional staff system is as complex as any military organization. In general, however, it can be broken down into two separate parts: the personal staff and the issue or committee staff.

The personal staff of a congressman or senator will generally be organized into the hierarchical structure shown on the previous page.

The precise titles of staff members will vary from office to office. "Personal aide" is sometimes used in preference to "secretary." "Professional staff" is often a surrogate for "legislative assistant." Whatever the titles, the roles of various staff members will usually follow the scheme outlined in the chart.

The Administrative Assistant

Administrative assistants (AAs), particularly on the House side, are almost always the most powerful people on the staff. Their role is not only to run the day-to-day operations of the congressional office, but to screen all issues on which the member must make decisions. They place priorities upon whom the member of Congress must see, which speeches she must give, and which constituents require attention. A good AA must have Machiavellian political instincts, as well as organizational ability, patience, charm, and, upon occasion, a nasty temper.

Administrative assistants are rarely issue-oriented. They have neither the time nor the inclination to learn the minutiae of legislative proposals. Their job is to reduce the hundreds of demands upon a congressman to a manageable number and present the member with clear-cut options for each issue they feel is worthy of the member's attention. Even in poorly run offices, it is difficult to present an issue effectively to the member if the AA has not already decided it is a matter the congressman should be concerned about. (Since Senate staffs are organizationally more complex, this function might be performed by a senior legislative assistant, leaving the AA to strictly administrative duties.)

Almost without exception, administrative assistants are more impressed by political reality than by the merits of a lobbyist's position. Therefore, when discussing issues with administrative assistants, always emphasize the politics of the member's district in explaining the facts of your case. An AA will be as concerned about the number of constituents who will be directly affected by your legislative proposals as he is about the details of your position. Your position's economic impact upon a member's district is also an important factor to emphasize when speaking with administrative assistants. Even if very few constituents might be directly affected, the dollar potential for a congressman's district should not be overlooked. Successful lobbyists will also try to emphasize the emotional impact of their proposals in the member's district. Even if the issue is not financially vital to the voters, it may be politically charged. For example, ecology issues, particularly on the West Coast, have a high visibility factor that is not necessarily related to the monetary costs or benefits to the constituencies. In these areas, environmentalists are extremely well organized and often tend to be one-issue voters.

One of the best ways to emphasize the political sensitivity of your issue is to suggest that the congressman's support for your position would be of substantial benefit to him. It is almost never appropriate to threaten a congressman, even indirectly. An administrative assistant—the alter ego of the member—will react in a similar way.

Among things that would attract an administrative assistant to your position are the following:

1. Suggest that the congressman's support would be widely publicized in your organization's newsletter. This is free publicity for the congressman. Since your group is sponsoring it, the publicity is almost guaranteed to be positive. Further, it effectively represents free political propaganda, which few congressman are apt to refuse.

2. Suggest that your organization could issue press releases welcoming the congressman's support. Such an offer costs little and is more likely to be picked up by the press than a statement from the member's own office. If the administrative assistant likes the idea, be sure to include the member's press aide in your planning.

3. Suggest to the administrative assistant that the member be invited to a well-publicized function in her district where your supporters would commend her. Congressmen and senators love these events, especially when they can be turned into photo opportunities. There are many other types of staged events that can serve as photo opportunities. An environmentalist group might stage a walk through an area they wish to have preserved as wilderness. Unions, companies, and businessmen might invite the member to their plants to speak directly to their workers. Railroads might invite members of Congress to sit in locomotive cabs. Angry neighbors of airports might present congressmen with earmuffs while standing at the end of a busy runway. The possibilities are endless, but be sure to invite the press and emphasize the photo opportunity nature of the event. You might also want to have one or two of your own photographers present to add an air of importance to the affair.

When trying to impress an administrative assistant, a temperate approach is usually the most successful. Of all the people on Capitol Hill, administrative assistants are least influenced by cheerleaders or harbingers of doom.

If an administrative assistant indicates general agreement with your approach, suggest that the details be worked out at the staff level and in consultation with the member. You should also brief the legislative assistant assigned to the project. If any of the publicity stunts are to be included as a price for the congressman's support, be sure to include the member's press aide in your future discussions.

Depending upon the office, the administrative assistant may be the most important person you see. Some AAs literally control their bosses. In other offices the AA's power is somewhat less. But there is no office in which you can afford to ignore them.

The Personal Secretary

Notwithstanding all the stories of congressional secretaries who can't dial a telephone (much less type), most Hill secretaries are competent, loyal, and dedicated. Although it is not unheard of for a congressman to dally with his personal secretary, this should not be considered the norm. And if they do indulge in this sort of activity, it is generally outside of their own staff.

Despite this lack of physical intimacy, the member's secretary is closest to him on a personal basis. She (I say *she* because almost all personal secretaries in the House and Senate are women, Congress being exempt from equal employment opportunity requirements as a practical matter) will be the one who arranges the congressman's day card. These day cards are carried by virtually every member and are usually three-by-five-inch index cards with the member's schedule for that day. The personal secretary will keep a duplicate copy of the day card in a slightly different format. Although she can sometimes be countermanded by the administrative assistant or the member, it is she who generally controls the member's schedule. She suggests which persons or groups the member should see, which events he will participate in, and even when he will take his vacation. Personal secretaries also keep close tabs on the relative importance of persons wanting to speak with the congressman. Some callers can get right through to the member; others will be routed through Alexandria, Egypt, and swallowed by the telephone system in Dundalk, New York.

Although personal secretaries are not charged with making policy decisions on specific political issues, they are the master sergeants of Capitol Hill. Nothing can be accomplished without them. You may not need their support, but you cannot afford their enmity. Make it a point to get to know the personal secretaries of all the members of Congress with whom you have regular dealings. Not only will they help you in relations with the congressman, but they will be an invaluable source of information on the congressman's preferences. They also know quite a bit about other offices on the Hill and, as you get to know them better, can be a prime source of gossip as well as hard facts.

Few people pay personal secretaries the respect they feel they deserve. For example, although many prefer to be called by their first names, there are some who deeply resent it. Be sensitive to this and follow the lead of the staff. If they refer to her as Ms. Brown, do so yourself until you get to know her better.

Personal secretaries can be extremely useful to a lobbyist in helping to arrange functions on the Hill. As a private citizen, you have no direct access to Hill facilities such as meeting rooms or committee areas. These can, however, be provided if requested by a member (whose account will be charged). If you would like to have a function in one of the three dozen Hill committee rooms or special party rooms, a congressman's private secretary can arrange this for you. In addition, she can be invaluable by running interference for you with the catering bureaucracy on the Hill and by making sure that the member you invited to your function will actually show up.

The Press Aide

In most senatorial and congressional offices, the press aide is not at all what you would expect. Usually press aides have no particular qualifications for their job other than having worked on the congressman's campaign staff. Often, in offices of junior members, the press aide serves two or three other functions—usually that of a legislative assistant. His main function is to write press releases about what a wonderful job the member of Congress is doing for her district.

The press aide also edits the congressman's newsletter to his constituents. This so-called newsletter is thinly disguised political propaganda designed to inform the electorate on the member's activities in Washington. It is usually a four- to eight-page pamphlet; until recently, it has always been written in the first person singular, and the congressman has been characteristically egotistical about his accomplishments on behalf of his constituency. These newsletters usually consider half a dozen issues and often have pictures of the congressman meeting with various groups. An extremely effective way to promote your issue is to have a feature article on it included in a congressmen's newsletter. It's free, it reaches over fifty thousand people by first-class mail, and it's the closest thing to a free lunch you'll find in Washington.

Press aides are overworked, underloved, and subject to unreasonable deadlines. This gives you a significant advantage in dealing with them. They are often delighted to virtually reprint a statement you gave them for the member. They may tinker with a few of the phrases, but generally they will leave your piece untouched.

In preparing a press statement for a congressman, the primary rule is to make sure it is individualized for that office. A press release prepared for one congressman should never be given to any other congressional office in the same form. Press releases are personalized by relating them to a member's district or committee activities. A reference to your group can also be tactfully inserted into the press statement.

The release you give to the press aide should be typed on plain bond paper in a standard format. This will enable the press aide to claim credit for preparing the release herself, but you will not have deceived the congressional office as to the origin of the document. This is important. If you feel that either the press aide or her office would regard this procedure as deceptive, be more straightforward. A sample press release is as follows:

FOR IMMEDIATE RELEASE

Congressman Bigelow Labels Round Earth Bill a Taxpayer Rip-Off

Washington, [date]. Congressman James T. Bigelow (D—Pa.) today labeled the Round Earth Amendments Bill "a taxpayer rip-off that would do nothing to promote science but would feed an already bloated federal bureaucracy." Speaking before the Flat Earth Society National Convention, the congressman said, "Certain people in this country want to get the government in the business of promoting their own ideology at taxpayer expense. I, for one, want no part of that." The congressman went on to say that he had consistently supported prudence in federal spending and saw government support for round earth theory as yet another example of government waste.

"Public funds are a public trust," said Bigelow. "They should not be used for any special interest group's purposes." The congressman warned the delegates that the round earth bill had considerable support in Congress, and pledging his continued opposition to this legislation, concluded, "If passage of this ill-conceived measure appears inevitable, I will do my best to assure that equivalent funds are appropriated to present the other point of view."

The Round Earth Amendments Bill would provide federal funds for instruction at the elementary and junior high school levels in round earth theory.

For further information contact Rob Greenspan, 555-6142.

The above example may appear a monument of hypocrisy, yet it is only a slightly altered version of an actual release from a congressional office. (Names, of course, have been changed to protect the innocent.) This is not an outrageous example of congressional press releases. Most are more cleverly written, but all have a singular purpose: to promote a particular issue and ultimately to promote the member himself.

Press aides are impressed if you can put them in touch with sympathetic reporters. Strange as it may seem, most congressmen have a difficult time getting their names in print on a regular basis. This is one of the press aide's main responsibilities. It is usually easier to get a press aide to agree to a meeting with a lobbying group than it is a reporter. After all, reporters need only call the congressional office if they want a story. You should use such meetings to get press coverage for *your* issue. A meeting will always be most effective if you have thoroughly briefed the press aide beforehand. An earnest statement expressing the congressman's support of your position can be very persuasive to a reporter, particularly if it is accompanied by a press release from the member's office.

Press aides who are good at their jobs will almost certainly know reporters from publications in the member's district. If you have strong constituent relations with the member, it is sometimes better if you contact the reporter first. Brief the reporter on your issue and express some doubt about the congressman's position. The reporter, if urged, will call the press aide. Given the Watergate mentality of most Washington stringers, they can usually intimidate a press aide into committing the congressman to a particular position. If you have played your cards carefully and honestly—the press aide (who is often cited as a "reliable source" in news stories) will commit the congressman to supporting your position in public. Even if the aide waffles, your issue will be brought to the member's attention. This approach can work to your benefit, but generally it is better policy not to try to intimidate press aides, but to work with them and convince them of the rectitude of your position.

The news media can be a powerful tool when used to your advantage. Congressional offices would rather support than oppose you insofar as the media are involved. Be *very* judicious in siccing a reporter on a congressional office. It is likely to backfire unless you have carefully briefed the press aide.

Remember, press aides, if played correctly, can be the most easily manipulated of all congressional staffers. They have inordinate demands placed upon them and are, in Tom Wolfe's parlance, the "flak catchers" of Capitol Hill. Anything you do to make their lives easier will be rewarded.

The Legislative Assistant

Legislative assistants (LAs) are the people with whom you should have the greatest contact on the Hill. These are experts on specific legislative issues. Their views will be translated into speeches for the congressman. Their opinions will usually determine the member's views on your subject. In short, they can make you or break you. Nothing can be more useful to a lobbyist than the sympathetic ear of a legislative assistant. Even if the LA is not as fully briefed on the matter as you are, his trust is the most important commodity you can have.

When dealing with an LA, as opposed to an AA, you can concentrate less on politics and more on facts. If the congressman's office is sympathetic to your position, do not be afraid to lay out all the facts— favorable and unfavorable—and work out an action plan with the LA. Your function is to distill the issue into a politically defensible position. During all your discussions, however, you should maintain one image: that of a provider. Although the LA has sources you cannot hope to duplicate (such as the Congressional Research Service), you should offer to undertake any research, grassroots action, dealings with the press, or other effort to promote your position. Unless the LA volunteers for a project, do not suggest that she perform any administrative or research function.

It is the LA to whom you will explain your issue and who will rely upon your additional information. The LAs can often intercede for you with the administrative assistants and the members themselves. If you have been successful in convincing them of the rectitude of your cause, they can even overcome opposition from above. LAs are essential to you. Forget them at your peril.

The Committee Staffs

Most Hill staffers do not work for members' personal staffs, but in the three dozen committees of the House and Senate. Some committee staffs number upward of fifty, and most have at least twenty-five professional and clerical employees. Although Hill committee staff members are supposed to be merely backup for the committee members, their jobs are intensely political. In most cases, senior committee staff members are appointed by the ranking senator or congressman serving on that committee. They are thus an adjunct to the congressman's or senator's personal staff and represent one of the fringe benefits of seniority.

The partisan makeup of the committee will dictate the number of majority and minority staff members it has. Thus the ranking majority member of a particular committee will have virtually exclusive authority in appointing his people to committee staffs for those committees he serves on. This seniority rule is not immutable. It is therefore useful to find out in advance the patronage of the committee staff member with whom you will be dealing. Judicious use of a congressman's or senator's name during your dealings with the committee staff member can be extremely useful.

When dealing with congressional committees, keep in mind the scope of their jurisdiction. Every committee on the Hill is extremely jealous of what it considers its territory and will demand that legislation be referred to it. Often bills are referred to one committee even though it seems that it would be more appropriate if they were considered by another committee. Do not be misled by the names of the committees. The Finance Committee, for example, has extensive jurisdiction over international trade matters—not the Foreign Relations Committee. Perhaps more confusing, several committees have concurrent jurisdiction over the same area. For example, the Senate Banking, Housing and Urban Affairs Committee shares jurisdiction over consumer issues with the Commerce, Science and Transportation Committee. The Energy and Natural Resources Committee of the Senate shares authority over power generation with the Environment and Public Works Committee. To make things even more complicated, the Appropriations Committees of both the House and the Senate have control of the purse strings for *all* government expenses and have subcommittees in each of the major areas whose prime jurisdiction lies with other committees.

To satisfy the egos of competing members of Congress and committee staffs, many pieces of legislation are concurrently or consecutively referred to two or more committees. This delays consideration of a proposed bill and can be used to your advantage if you are opposing legislation. In fact, one of your initial tactics, should you be attempting to defeat a particular bill, is to contact your sources within committees to which the legislation *might* have been referred and suggest to them that another committee is handling matters that rightfully should be considered by them. You can often get consecutive or concurrent referral of the bill. Even if it passes in one committee, you can bottle it up in another. Conversely, if you are supporting a particular piece of legislation and it is assigned to a committee on which you have few allies, it can be beneficial for you to get it referred to another committee on which you have a substantial number of friends.

As when dealing with the personal staffs of congressmen and senators, your relations with committee staffs should be characterized by openness and honesty. You should, however, expect to be much more technical with the committee staffs than you were with the individual member's personal staff. You are now dealing with the experts on the intent, substance and implementation of legislation. The vague language you might have used with a congressman's AA or LA will not suffice at the committee staff level. In many cases you will be speaking with people who actually wrote the existing legislation in the field; you cannot impress them with generalities. They will be interested in your specific proposals and the precise language you would like to implement or defeat.

Each congressional committee staff will have several lawyers on the payroll, but even the nonlegal staff members tend to think in legalistic terms. You should prepare yourself for meetings with this group of people by reading and rereading the existing law, the proposed changes, and any backup material you can find.

As with the personal staff, your job is to assist the committee staff in preparing the desired changes. To do this you need to know more about the subject than they do. Although this might seem to be a monumental task, given the fact that they spend their entire lives considering the subject matter in which you are interested, they probably will not have focused upon the technical aspects of your particular piece of legislation. There are only thirty committees to handle more than a million pages of proposed legislation, so staffers simply do not have the time to give it the attention you can provide.

The Initial Contact

In approaching the committee staff members, it is desirable to isolate the individual responsible for the legislation on a subcommittee basis first. Subcommittee designations can be found in the *Congressional Directory*, the *Congressional Yellow Book,* or other sources listed in Chapter 19. Once you have determined the appropriate subcommittee, call that office and ask the first person with whom you speak which staff member is responsible for your issue. Invariably the first information you receive will be incorrect. You should, however, call the person to whom you are referred, who will refer you to someone else. After two or three telephone calls you should finally arrive at the right desk. When you speak to the appropriate committee staff member, give him or her a brief outline of the issue you would like to discuss, and arrange for a personal meeting. As soon as you hang up the phone, check out the person with whom you spoke in one of the sources listed in Chapter 19. Remember, each staff member generally has a counterpart staffer in the same committee from the other political party. You will want to speak with that person at some point as well. Arrange a meeting with the committee staff member whom you called. Lunch is a traditional Washington introduction.

Until recently, Capitol Hill was a wasteland of fast food establishments and second-rate cafeterias. During the past several years, however, a number of good restaurants have opened within walking distance of both the House and Senate. Reservations are recommended at some of these. Try to arrive a little early for lunch; most of the restaurants will be about a ten-minute walk from the congressional office buildings.

While you are at lunch, give the staff member only a very general outline of your position, and try to find out how much she knows about the issue under consideration. You do not want to condescend to a person who already knows more than you do about the subject; nor do you want to overwhelm someone who has never heard of your issue. Feel the staff member out on a subject related to your own; try to develop a personal rapport. After lunch, decide whether it would be advantageous to go back to the aide's office with her. Be extremely sensitive to the aide's schedule. Some staffers don't have the luxury of an extended lunch. You may also find appointments canceled or curtailed because of changes in the legislative schedule. In short, don't be pushy. If it is propitious, and you decide to accompany the LA back to her office, you should be ready to lay out your whole case in less than fifteen minutes. By this time, you should have determined how much the staff member knows about your subject and the best areas to explore in the future. Almost invariably, you will find that there are several issues on which the staff member is not fully briefed. Be sure to take careful notes on these. (Many lobbyists do this on a legal pad. Although it's bulky, you can put a lot of information on it and it looks official.) On every issue for which the staff member requests additional information, be sure to respond very promptly, usually within twenty-four hours. You should also make it a habit to get back in touch with the staff member on at least a weekly basis, and preferably every third or fourth day. Remember, you're going to be discussing the technical aspects of your issue with this person; this can't be accomplished in one day.

You should also be in touch with the other party's staff member. Be very sensitive in this matter. Going to the minority party can sometimes be helpful if the ranking majority member on the subcommittee is either not interested in or is opposed to your position; but minority members rarely have the power of a majority party subcommittee member. In any event, you should be sure to contact the minority staff member, if only to keep him informed of what you're doing.

Senate and House committee staff members will judge your position more on its merits than anyone else you speak to on the Hill. They will be the most critical of your statistics and will have no difficulty checking your figures. They can also be your greatest ally in getting your issue appropriately addressed. A committee staff member who believes that your position has merit will rarely encounter a technical argument from the member's personal staff. If you have done your political homework with the personal staff, everything should go smoothly.

In your discussions with the committee staff, you will want to meet with staff counsel who, upon instruction of a congressional office, will assist you in preparing actual legislative language. Even if you think you have done an adequate job in drafting the language, or are actively opposing legislation, it is still a good idea to spend some time with legislative counsel. Although they are among the most important people on Capitol Hill, the people who actually write the laws, they are ignored by most lobbyists. They sincerely appreciate any attention they receive, and your time with them will be well spent.

Eleven

★ ★ ★ ★ ★

The Congressional Visit

★ ★ ★ ★ ★

In order to become the master, the politician poses as the servant.

—Charles de Gaulle

The tradition most associated with Washington lobbying is the actual pressing of flesh with a member of Congress. Although few congressional lobbying campaigns ignore this tradition, seldom has success resulted from a concentration on face-to-face meetings to the exclusion of other lobbying methods, particularly good staff contacts and adequate homework.

Whom to See

Most of the real work of a lobbying campaign is done at the staff level and through your letter-writing and grassroots campaigns. It is essential, however, that you be in *direct* personal contact with your congressional allies. You should also plan on seeing "swing" members whether they agree with your position or not. (A "swing" congressman is one who can either control a number of other votes or whose own vote may decide a particular issue.) This includes committee and subcommittee chairmen, ranking minority members of all appropriate committees and subcommittees, and any other members of Congress who are known to have an active interest in your position. Finally, you owe a visit to members of Congress with constituencies that are particularly favorable to your position.

When visiting members of Congress who are not directly concerned with your issue in their committees, you should go out of your way to be sure that they are aware of a vital constituent interest in your matter. It is best if you can include one of their constituents in the group that meets with the member, but *never* permit a powerful but uninformed constituent to speak for your group even in the confines of a member's office. The constituent in question should always be accompanied by a person who is adequately briefed on all the issues and who is capable of following up on any questions that may arise during the course of the meeting. Before meeting with any member, you should prepare a list of all members of Congress with whom you wish to meet. In most cases, you can develop a "must-see" list and a secondary list of members whom it would be important but not essential to have on your side.

The Summary Sheet

For each of the congressmen and senators on your list, you should prepare a summary sheet. This will include data on the members; almost all of this information is available from public sources, but the emphasis here will be on your particular issue. The summary sheet should include analyses of what *other* interest groups think about the Member. Dozens of lobbying organizations "rank" members according to how they vote on issues of concern to that organization. The weight given to each vote varies from group to group, and various organizations choose the most "important" topics themselves. Thus, the ranking given by one group may not be directly comparable to another group's grading policies. You should carefully note precisely what criteria are used by each group before making any sweeping judgments. Despite this problem, a review of the rankings can provide a general idea of the political proclivities of a Member, and is a useful tool for preliminary analysis. A sample summary sheet might be as follows:

Congresswoman Sybil Simpatico (D—NM)
Second District

Biography

Born: March 12, 1930, Belmont, N.J.; Home: Lovington, N.M.; B.S.: Harvard, 1951; J.D.: Yale, 1954; Married, three children; Catholic; Career: Securities Exchange Commission, 1955-58; Nasty, Poor, Brutish, and Short (law firm), Santa Fe, 1956-62 (Partner, 1960); N.M. Senate, 1961-64; elected U.S. House of Representatives, 1964; Committees: Interior and Insular Affairs; Subcommittees: Mine and Mining, Oversight/Special Investigations, Water and Power Resources.

Ratings

ADA	COPE	ACA	NTU	NAB	NSI*
20	34	63	50	46	60

---

* Organizations providing ratings include:

ADA—Americans for Democratic Action, 1411 K Street, N.W., Washington, D.C. 20005. This is generally regarded as the premier liberal political organization in the United States, and its ratings reflect explicitly liberal values.

COPE—AFL-CIO Committee on Political Education, 815 16th Street, N.W., Washington, D.C. 20006. This rating reflects the point of view of the nation's largest organized labor organization.

PC—Public Citizen, 133 C Street, S.E., Washington, D.C. 20003. This organization, founded by Ralph Nader in 1971, tends to reflect his views.

RIPON—The Ripon Society, 800 18th Street, N.W., Washington, D.C. 20006. This is a group of people who identify themselves as liberal Republicans.

NFU—National Farmers Union, 1012 14th Street, N.W., Washington, D.C. 20005. This farmers' organization tends to be closer in views to Democrats than Republicans, in contrast to, among others, the American Farm Bureau Federation, which does not issue ratings.

CFA—Consumers' Federation of America, 1012 14th Street, N.W., Washington, D.C. 20005. This group describes itself as pro consumer.

NAB—National Associated Businessmen, Inc., 1000 Connecticut Avenue, N.W., Washington, D.C. 20036. This group works for economy in government, concentrating on domestic spending. It regularly issues a "Watchdog of the Treasury" award.

NSI—National Security Index of the American Security Council, 499 S. Capitol, S.W., Washington, D.C. 20003. This index reflects support for or opposition to major defense expenditures and military programs.

ACA—Americans for Constitutional Action, 955 L'Enfant Plaza, S.W., Washington, D.C. 20024. This is a group as explicitly conservative as the ADA is liberal.

NTU—National Taxpayers Union, 1521 Pennsylvania Avenue, S.E., Washington, D.C. 20003. This group wants to cut government spending and compiles a rating based on every spending vote in Congress during the year.

Key Votes on Flat Earth Issues
Special Department of Education Appropriations For
National Science Foundation Special Grants Against
NASA Propaganda For
Local School Control For
HEW Appropriations For

Constituent Contacts

1. Alistair Greely, Albuquerque Flat Earth Society: Division Four (fifty members); thirty confirmed letters to congressmen (February–March)

2. Jennifer Bell, major contributor Las Cruces, N.M. member: Flat Earth Society: Division Fourteen

3. Janet Wilenska, Chairman, Flat Earth Caucus, N.M. Democratic Party member: Flat Earth Society, Local 31

Staff
John Border (555–2125) (L.A. Constituent Services)
Contact: Carol Matheson

The next page of the summary sheet should outline your presentation to this particular Congresswoman, stressing the factors you wish to discuss with her. You should tailor the summary sheet for the particular issues that will affect her vote, with particular emphasis upon constituent relationships and local issues.

Arranging a Visit

After you have prepared your summary sheet and contacted your constituent members, you should arrange for a meeting with the member of Congress by telephoning her appointments secretary. You can either get in touch with the secretary directly or through one of your staff contacts. If possible, the meeting should be arranged at a time when the member's committee is not scheduled for a session and should emphasize the proposed presence of her constituent at the meeting. Tell the staff member with whom you speak that you will take no more than fifteen minutes of the member's time. You should also be sure to check with the staffer so he can clear his calendar as well. You will want to include him in the meeting with his boss. After you have arranged a time, be sure to coordinate this with those of your members who will be meeting with the congresswoman. All these arrangements should take place at least a week prior to the actual appointment.

Staff Contact

For practical as well as political reasons, you must be sure that the persons with whom you have been dealing on the congressional staff are fully briefed on the reasons for the meeting. It should not appear that you are attempting to go over the staff member's head in meeting with the congresswoman, merely that you have a constituent with a personal message for her. You must handle the situation with extreme diplomacy. Remember, the staff member will be advising the congresswoman on your issue. You cannot afford to alienate staff members at any stage, and a sure way to do so is to embarrass them in front of their superior. Before the meeting, the staff member will have already briefed the congresswoman. When you arrive at the office, the congresswoman will have a very good idea of the issues you wish to raise, as well as a proposed plan of action. You should work with the staff member on briefing papers that he will give to the congresswoman.

In some offices, the staff member will want to have a dossiers— files containing detailed records—on the constituent you will be bringing, on you and on your group. You should provide these upon request.

Except in the most unusual circumstances, you should never arrange for a meeting with a congressman without first briefing the relevant staff members. Failure to do so is not merely a breach of protocol; it can be destructive to your entire presentation. If, once the meeting is over and you have left the room, the congressman turns to his staff aide and says, "What the hell was that all about?"— and the staff member doesn't know—you might just as well have stayed home.

What to Say, How to Say It

Your meeting is arranged; you have briefed the staff member, prepared your summary sheets, and made sure your constituent is aware of the issues. Now you must explain your position to the member of Congress herself.

Be sure to arrive at the member's office about five minutes early. Although you may have a specific appointment time, Hill schedules are infuriatingly flexible. Members are called for record votes, committee meetings, or constituent hand-holding and have a dozen other distractions. You cannot afford to have your own tardiness derail your meeting. Further, to maintain a good reputation with members of your own group, you cannot afford to keep them waiting in a member's anteroom for longer than fifteen to twenty minutes.

When you arrive, first ask to see the legislative assistant who will be sitting in on the meeting. You should discuss with the LA any last-minute developments and introduce him to the other people in your delegation. When you're ushered into the member's office, the staff member should be given the opportunity to introduce you if you have not met the member before. If you have, take the initiative and say how glad you are to see her again (stressing the *again*), and introduce her to your other delegation members. Next tell the member how much you have appreciated her staffer's assistance (the staff member, of course, smiling modestly). Be sure to do this even if the staff member has been sitting on his hands for the past six weeks. You're not necessarily thanking him for his past assistance, but praise is fertilizer for future relationships.

Give the member a one-page summary of your issue and your position. If the staffer has done his job, the member will already have been briefed on most of the salient points; but you should stress the areas outlined in your summary sheet. (Be sure *not* to give the member the summary sheet concerning her background described in this chapter.) If you have a constituent attending this meeting, he should do most of the introductory presentation; you should merely fill in as necessary. If there is no constituent available, you should still present your case to the member in terms of her constituency, emphasizing those areas in which she has expressed a particular concern and slanting your argument to her political predilections.

During the course of the interview, be sure to have a legal pad on your lap and take careful notes of both the points made and questions asked of you. Invariably, the staff member will be keeping similar notes; you will want to compare these after the meeting.

Never under any circumstances should you attempt to intimidate, threaten, or bribe the member or make promises you cannot keep. Most members of Congress simply will not respond to threats, bribes, unsupported allegations, or skulduggery. You should not, however, attempt to be formalistic about your presentation. You and your constituent should be straightforward, frank, and explicit. You should present your case and ask the member in specific terms to commit herself to your objectives. This is a briefing session; but, more important, you are attempting to get her to commit to a favorable or at least neutral position on your issue. Remind her of her past votes and the issues involved in them. Stress the factual and political factors which you feel are most important to her, taking your lead from the staff member present. If someone in your delegation gets out of line, cut him off short; you cannot afford the enmity of a congresswoman for personal reasons. Above all, keep your comments short. You should be able to present your entire case in fifteen minutes unless the congresswoman herself extends the interview by asking questions.

Be polite, be succinct, be aggressive. Don't be awed by a member's title. Since you have only fifteen minutes, you should not be distracted by secondary issues; stick to the subject. Members of Congress have a penchant for diverting the conversation from uncomfortable subjects; don't let that happen to you. At the conclusion of the interview, be sure to leave a list of all names, titles, and addresses of your people so that the member can assess your importance and write follow-up letters if appropriate. In this regard, you should not only leave a typed list of all persons attending the meeting, but business cards as well. Often the members of your delegation will not have formal cards; but no matter how cursory your lobbying effort, you should have them made for yourself. These should be distributed not only at congressional meetings, but at any session you have with staff members.

A business card need not be elaborate. Your name, organization, address, and telephone number on a simple white card is sufficient. These can be printed at minimal cost in Washington and are de rigueur for any remotely serious lobbyist. Even if you have ample funds, multicolored or unique cards do not justify the expense. If you wish to be more elaborate, a heavy, engraved card is preferable to a flashy foldout.

Follow-Up

After the meeting, you and all of the other participants in the interview should write thank-you letters to the member. Separate thank-you letters should also be written to the staff members who participated in the interview. If you have been dealing with a particular staff member who was not able to attend the meeting, you should send him a letter informing him of the meeting and the relative success you achieved. In your thank-you letters, be sure to restate the basic points you made during the meeting itself and ask the member of Congress to take action on your behalf. A sample letter might read as follows:

The Honorable Sybil Simpatico
United States House of Representatives
Washington, D.C. 20515

Dear Congresswoman Simpatico:

On behalf of myself and the entire Flat Earth Society, I want to thank you again for your courtesy in seeing us on September 23. All of us, and in particular Jennifer Bell, express their deepest appreciation for your courtesy. We were especially encouraged by your expression of support for flat earthism and opposition to the round earth bill.

This, in our view, is an extremely serious matter and is likely to result in a very close vote on the House floor in the near future. The round earth amendments are not only an ill-disguised attempt by federal bureaucrats to dictate the scientific theology of local school districts, but a consummate waste of taxpayers' funds. Further, as you are aware, a majority of voters in your district steadfastly oppose the philosophy inherent in round earthism. We hope we can count on you to use whatever influence you have to defeat this bill in committee; failing that, it can be beaten on the floor. As you requested, I have enclosed additional information regarding the impact of round earthism on the Department of Education's appropriations for next year. If you need any additional data, please do not hesitate to contact me.

Sincerely,

Linda Borcum
For the Flat Earth Society
cc: John Border

About a week after you have had your meeting with the member of Congress, you should call the member's staff to make sure the member has performed the tasks she promised. This should be done in a very low-key manner: *no one* likes to be nagged, but nag you must if you are to be successful. As soon as the congresswoman or senator acts on her promise, you should be sure to write even more effusive thank-you letters and tell your constituents that the member has kept her promise.

Meeting a member of Congress, although the most dramatic and traditional form of lobbying, is only a small part of a complete lobbying program. Nevertheless it is essential, and you should be sure to include it in your plans.

Twelve

A Sympathizer would seem to imply a certain degree of benevo-lent feeling. Nothing of the kind. It signifies a ready-made accomplice in any species of political villainy.
—Thomas Love Peacock, *Gryll Grange*

As noted in Chapter 3, identification of your friends and opponents should be one of your first objectives in a lobbying campaign. It is, however, only half the job. You must turn this knowledge to your advantage. Although you will not be dealing closely with your enemies, you should have a good working relationship with your allies. This chapter focuses primarily on how to treat your friends both on the Hill and downtown.

Government Agencies

Your most valuable allies in any congressional matter may not be in the Congress at all. There is virtually no legislation that does not affect some government department, bureau, agency, or commission. Almost without exception, these administrative bodies dearly love to see their scope of authority expanded. Such legislation means increased budgets, higher prestige, and more influence in the power struggles of official Washington. This being the case, you can generally count on the support of the agency that would be charged with administering your legislation. Conversely, legislation transferring or even abolishing existing programs is likely to meet with fervent opposition from the agency currently charged with its administration. Washington is so complex and the bureaucracy so huge, however, that one agency's discomfiture almost automatically causes elation at another branch of the administration. If a program currently administered by the Department of Agriculture is killed, bureaucrats at such disparate agencies as the Department of Housing and Urban Development, Health and Human Services, and even the State Department sometimes secretly rejoice. Just because your objective might be to *repeal* existing legislation, do not despair of finding allies within the government agencies.

Although several attempts have been made to prohibit government agencies from actively lobbying for or against specific legislation, such laws are a mere chimera. Most government agencies maintain a "congressional liaison" staff, which is but another term for lobbyist in bureaucratese. These congressional liaison officers perform virtually identical services as independent lobbyists, but have vast resources at their disposal, including platoons of researchers who can churn out position papers at the drop of a hat. These liaison people are familiar with all issues related to their agency and often have years of practical experience on the Hill. If you can harness these energies for *your* purposes, you will have gained thousands of dollars' worth of lobbying at the taxpayers' expense.

Your research should have uncovered the agencies most likely to come to your aid. You should approach the target agencies gingerly. Most bureaucrats are intensely suspicious of outsiders and, whether they admit it or not, secretly believe no one but themselves should really have the right to recommend changes in their agency's operation. This initial suspicion can be dispelled if you emphasize that your interest relates only to final objectives and not necessarily to the manner in which the agency administers the law. Bureaucrats are a much-maligned breed and are as susceptible to criticism (and praise) as anyone else. It is almost always profitable to tell bureaucrats that you sympathize with their position. One tack is to suggest to them that they don't have the current authority to accomplish their mission and your legislation would give them that authority.

In approaching an administrative agency, you should be thoroughly familiar with its organizational structure. Each agency maintains a schematic diagram of its internal chain of command. These are available from the public affairs office of the agency concerned. You should get a copy of this chart for each agency that you intend to approach before making your initial overtures to them.

Your target should not ordinarily be the congressional liaison office of the agency concerned, but the subdivision of the agency that is currently charged or would be charged with administering the program contemplated in your legislation. The agency's congressional liaison office rarely has the authority to make policy decisions; its marching orders are passed through an elaborate chain of command that starts with the section of the agency ultimately responsible for administering the legislation. If you succeed in securing the agency's endorsement for your proposal, and it is subsequently cleared through the labyrinth of the bureaucracy, you should work closely with the congressional liaison offices of the agencies concerned. In many cases, they will have contacts and expertise on the Hill that take years to develop. Further, seldom would legislation having a direct effect upon an agency be introduced and then the formal position of the agency not be requested. You can be instrumental in influencing the statements made by the agency if you have previously cleared the concept through the appropriate bureaucratic channels.

In a similar vein, the administration as a whole is often asked its position on pending legislation. The decision as to whether the executive branch will support or oppose particular legislation is often the subject of interagency review. Even if "your" agency is not able to prevail in this review process, at least you can delay an administration edict, encourage watered-down opposition, or promote neutrality. In any event, having one or more government departments on your side of a lobbying effort can improve your chances of success. Given the minimal cost of approaching the agencies, the enormous resources they can bring to bear on your side of an issue and the minimal risk involved if you have done your homework, a partnership with a federal agency is almost always to be recommended.

A note of caution: because of their highly formalized structure, decision making within government agencies is ponderous and usually frustrating. Do not expect to get an affirmative decision from any agency overnight. Even when a decision apparently *has* been made, its implementation can be delayed. The orders may not go out to the congressional liaison officers for days or even weeks after a position has been taken by the policy makers within the department. If you recognize these factors in advance, you are less likely to be disappointed when the agency does not act as expeditiously as you would like. Conversely, if you are opposing the position of an agency, the very ponderousness of its decision making can work to your advantage. You can line up your allies before your "establishment" opposition can even get its troops ready to march. Despite the institutional problems of dealing with agencies, their support is worth going after.

Other Interest Groups

If you have done your homework, you also should have identified a number of potential allies outside of the government (see Chapter 3). You should have reviewed all groups with any interest in your ultimate objectives, whether or not they have traditionally opposed your positions. Do not overlook any opportunities for alliance merely because you have had quarrels on other issues or the other group appears philosophically at odds with your beliefs. In approaching other interest groups, you should stress objectives rather than the philosophical motivations of your newfound allies. Your—and their—reasons for wanting to accomplish a particular goal are, for the purpose of a lobbying campaign, tactical rather than strategic considerations. If you succeed in gaining the alliance of another group, you should very carefully establish the ground rules. These should be specified in a memorandum of understanding that incorporates at least the following factors:

1. a clear statement of the ultimate objective (such as passage or defeat of a particular piece of legislation)

2. a list of individuals from each group who will be participating in the lobbying campaign

3. a statement of responsibility for preparation of position papers, resource books, and all other written material to be used in the campaign

4. establishment of procedures by which contacts, error correction, and so on will be implemented

5. formation of a review committee for editing materials to be used in the campaign

You will avoid all sorts of confrontations and misunderstandings if your relationship with your allies is spelled out in detail *before* you undertake substantive work together.

Confrontation often arises when allies think up different ways to accomplish the same objective. The group you're working with can probably draw upon different strengths than those available to your group. You should not insist that they merely adopt your methods; rather, give them the freedom to take advantage of their strengths. Although you may be somewhat uncomfortable with some of their arguments, so long as they cannot be challenged on the basis of accuracy you should bite your lip and let it go. The only danger here is inconsistent arguments, but these can usually be worked out when editing the memorandum of understanding. The goals and procedures worked out early in your relationship should be reviewed on a regular basis.

Many groups may want to join you, particularly if it appears that you are going to be successful in your lobbying efforts; but you should be sure that all parties shoulder their share of the burden. It is one thing to work with allies, quite another to carry them.

Members of Congress

The body that you are lobbying—the Congress—can be your greatest source of support. Not only can members vote on your side of the issue, but they also can be instrumental in convincing others to do so. Congressional offices have myriad lobbying devices, many of which are unavailable to outside lobbyists. Among these are the following.

"Dear Colleague" Letters

A letter signed by one or more members or their colleagues is a traditional vehicle for expressing views on Capitol Hill. Often you will have an opportunity to either advise or actually prepare these "dear colleague" letters. Although rather common, they still carry a great deal of weight, particularly if you can get respected members to sign them or if you can attract congressmen and senators of disparate views. Sometimes several "dear colleague" letters, each emphasizing a different aspect of your issue, are preferable to a single note with scores of erudite signatures.

Caucuses, Committees, and Party Organizations

Members of Congress have direct access to various restricted forums. They can make their views known in groups to which you would ordinarily be denied access. If a member is committed to your cause, you can suggest that she use all such privileges to promote your position.

Other Interest Groups

It is rare that a lobbyist or special interest group would flatly refuse a request from a congressman. After all, the lobbyist has a lot of favors to ask the member in return. If you need a favor from someone, particularly in the private sector, one of the best ways to approach the person is to have a friendly congressman make the initial contact.

Log Rolling

Whatever the didactic skills of your friendly congressman, his ability to convince his colleagues of the objective merits of your issue may be somewhat less impressive than his political power. Although trading votes may seem somewhat sordid, it is a tradition in American politics and is just as much a part of lobbying as a letter-writing campaign. If a member feels strongly about your issue, he can use all manner of resources to convince other congressmen to go along with him. These range from straight vote trading to using his influence as chairman of a committee or subcommittee, caucus, state delegation, party post, and so on. If you secure a member of Congress as your lobbying ally, you should be prepared to help him in any way he requires, such as preparation of position papers or research. You will not be able to control what a congressman says or does nearly as well as you would your own people. This can be embarrassing, but the risk is worth it. A friendly member can do much more good than harm to your cause.

Endorsements

Some lobbying campaigns spend a great deal of time and effort attempting to get as many groups as possible to endorse their positions. Although endorsements are worthwhile, they are often highly overrated. A long list of organizations supporting your position can be impressive and gives a certain amount of credibility to your cause; but unless the groups endorsing you are also willing to do active lobbying, you cannot expect their names to carry the day. It is better to have three groups that will give you time, effort, money, and man-power than thirty that will merely lend you the use of their name. Given limited resources, you should spend much more time attempting to convince people to *work* with you than to merely approve of what you are saying.

Nevertheless, a long list of endorsing organizations can be helpful, particularly in areas where you are not especially strong. In seeking endorsements, you should make it very clear to the groups contacted that you want to use their names publicly. It can be devastating if a group that you claim has endorsed your position subsequently repudiates the endorsement. This can usually be avoided by good communication from the outset. You should also keep the leaders of any group that endorses you aware of the manner in which you use their name, making sure that you send them copies of all documents in which their name appears. If they have declined to do more than merely sanction the use of their organization's title, it is not generally necessary for you to clear the text of every single document with them. You should, however, be very judicious in not misrepresenting their endorsement. You should be particularly careful not to cover areas that were not discussed in your preliminary conversations.

Conversely, your group should *never* endorse a lobbying campaign sponsored by another organization unless you plan to take an active part in the promotion of that group's cause. From your perspective, endorsements gain you no followers, and the political points you may get with other groups are ephemeral at best. Finally, your future credibility should never be entrusted to another organization unless you have the ability to control statements made in your name.

Thirteen

★ ★ ★ ★ ★

Money

★ ★ ★ ★ ★

Get thee glass eyes;
And, like a scurvy politician,
To seem to see the thing thou dost not ...
　　　　　　　　—William Shakespeare, *King Lear*

The Law

To be a successful lobbyist you must be able to effectively raise funds for your cause and utilize those funds propitiously. Before you embark on a lobbying campaign, you should familiarize yourself with the laws that apply to the regulation of money. This is the "mother's milk" of politics and is clearly the most controversial.

Federal regulation of income and expense to influence political causes has always attempted to steer a narrow path between preventing corruption and infringing upon First Amendment rights. While (almost) everyone is opposed to graft, most would also agree that an outright ban on using money to express a political opinion is a constitutionally protected right. Zoning laws aside, few would disagree that, for example, putting a sign in your yard advocating the election (or defeat) of a particular candidate is clearly within a citizen's constitutional prerogative. The Congress has wrestled many times with this conundrum, vacillating between mere "transparency laws," which require divulging the source of funds and their expenditure, to outright bans on certain types of spending. The most recent revision of the lobbying finance laws was enacted in 1995 (the Lobbying Disclosure Act). This law made sweeping changes in prior regulations, and creates vast minefields for the unwary. As of the date of this book, it is still unclear whether all of this law's provisions will pass constitutional muster, but in the meantime, it would be prudent for potential lobbyists to assume that the statute is indeed valid, and to become extremely familiar with its provisions. A complete copy of this act can be found in Appendix A. Its main provisions are as follows:

1. Unlike prior legislation, the disclosure act applies to the executive branch as well as the Congress. The act has extensive provisions concerning the limits of permissible contacts and extensive reporting requirements depending upon the nature of communications with designated individuals, who is making such representations, and the content of the communication itself. For the first time, the act also covers even state government officials in certain circumstances.

2. Although the act purports to regulate only "professional" lobbyists, the definition of "lobbying" that triggers the most complex regulations starts at $5,000 for a "lobbying firm" and $20,000 for an organization. While these might seem like generous exemptions, these amounts relate to almost any activity related to attempting to influence public policy—not just the actual contacts with public officials.

Failure to abide by the act, including its voluminous reporting requirements, can lead to severe penalties (up to $50,000). Even if you do not believe you are covered, either because of the "threshold" amounts noted above, or because your group arguably fits within the definition of organizations specifically noted in the text (such as churches and certain other tax-exempt groups), you should pay careful attention to the act's requirements. It is very easy, for example, for an otherwise innocent group to raise and spend more than $20,000 on what might be construed as "lobbying activities," and be instantly covered. Further, the precise scope of the exemptions is likely to remain hazy for years to come, and *you* do not want to be a test case.

In addition to statutory law noted above, both the House and the Senate have complex ethics rules that limit the amounts each body's member may receive in the way of gifts and so on. These rules are constantly changing in response to real or perceived lapses on the part of the members.

The Federal Election Campaign Act contains provisions regarding contributions made to influence the result of an election. The act defines an "independent expenditure" as "[a]n expenditure by a person expressly advocating the election or defeat of a clearly identified candidate which is made without cooperation or consultation with any candidate, or any authorized committee or agent of such candidate, and which is not made in concert with or at the request or suggestion of any candidate, or any authorized committee or agent of such candidate."

Other provisions of the Federal Election Campaign Act limit the amount of contributions that can be made to a particular candidate or political committee. Section 441(a) states:

(1) No person shall make contributions—

   (A) to any candidate and his authorized political committees with respect to any election for Federal office which, in the aggregate, exceed $1,000; or

   (B) to the political committees established and maintained by a national political party, which are not the authorized political committees of any candidate, in any calendar year which, in the aggregate, exceed $20,000; or

   (C) to any other political committee in any calendar year which, in the aggregate, exceed $5,000.

It is also illegal for an individual to make contributions aggregating more than twenty-five thousand dollars in any calendar year.

Political committees, on the other hand, have much less stringent limitations imposed upon them with respect to contributions. The establishment and operations of a political committee are explicitly delineated in the Federal Election Campaign Act. Before you consider setting one up, however, you would be well advised not only to familiarize yourself with the law, but also to speak to an attorney.

(2) A political committee that contributes to more than one candidate cannot make contributions—

   (A) to any candidate and his authorized political committee with respect to any election for Federal office which, in the aggregate, exceed $5,000;

(B) to the political committees established and maintained by a national political party, which are not the authorized political committees of any candidate, in any calendar year, which, in the aggregate exceed $15,000; or

(C) to any other political committee in any calendar year, which in the aggregate, exceed $5,000.

Except for very specific situations, the campaign act prohibits a corporation from making a contribution or expenditure in connection with any election to any political office.

Gifts to Congressmen and Staffs

Disregard what you may have heard about members of Congress on the take. Leave it up to the FBI and crooks to attempt to buy influence in Washington. With the exception of contributions to congressional campaigns discussed on pages 128–137, you should be very reticent in giving either gifts or money to congressmen and their staffs. Many offices will simply not accept gifts; others will do so only under extremely restricted conditions. There are, however, several types of gifts to congressmen that are accepted lobbying tactics. These include the following.

Lunches

Lunch is a Washington tradition. Few congressmen or staff members will refuse to allow you to pick up the check for lunch. Although Washington restaurants are somewhat expensive (forty dollars for two people is not unheard of), some members of Congress and congressional staff members who would never consider taking a ten-dollar gratuity may accept a lunch. Be careful here, however, since the ethics rules of both the House and the Senate may prohibit buying even a hamburger for a staffer. Be sure you know your rule before you offer.

Books

For some reason books are not looked upon as gifts if they relate to your issue. Even expensive coffee-table books are routinely accepted by some of the most fastidious congressional staff members if they appear to have a nexus with the lobbyist's cause. For example, a book on wilderness might be gladly accepted by a congressman or senator who has assisted you in a land-use matter.

Gifts Under Five Dollars

The cut-off point between a gift and a bribe is at the five-dollar level (you can never be accused of bribing a congressman for what amounts to cab fare). You will have little occasion to actually give a member or one of her staffers cash; but the gifts of pens, pencils, and paperweights with a value of five dollars or so is routine in Washington. Even if the value is slightly over five dollars, you should not have a problem. Beware, however, of giving away radios, television sets, or the like; that is the fastest way of making it into Jack Anderson's column, and *that* you don't need.

Awards

Congressmen love to receive awards to adorn their offices. Dozens of groups routinely bestow awards upon members of Congress who have supported their views. Sometimes, these awards are elaborate (and expensive) plaques extolling the virtues of the member. As long as the award is not cash or a useful consumer item, don't worry too much about cost—within the bounds of good taste. Obviously, for example, a solid-gold loving cup worth fifteen thousand dollars would not be appropriate.

Liquor

Particularly at Christmastime, congressional offices seem to appreciate holiday spirit. As long as you don't overdo it, liquor is generally acceptable at that time of year. Usually it is used for office parties, the cost of which would otherwise have to come out of the member's budget. Although some lobbyists used to give away entire cases to senators and congressmen, you should limit yourself to one or two bottles. There is much less chance of criticism about a bottle of Scotch than a whole case of Jack Daniel's. Even here, however, use *extreme* caution. The new ethics rules have almost dried up the torrent of booze that flowed in former years. Now many congressional offices will not accept even a bottle of beer.

Models, Samples, and So On

Many industrial trade associations routinely distribute models or samples of their products to constituent congressmen. Although these models and samples are sometimes worth hundreds of dollars, they are rarely functional. When you get to the Hill you will see such objects displayed in congressional offices, so there obviously is not much resistance to them.

Other more suspicious gifts are free travel, hunting or golfing trips, theater tickets, and stock. If you would really like to give such a gift, and the member indicates that he is willing to accept it, you should first protect both yourself and the member by having one of his staff members check with the Senate or House Ethics Committee on its appropriateness. The question should be phrased in terms of *how* the member could accept your proffered gift within the law, and a letter stating an opinion should be requested from the committee. If the committee indicates that the gift is acceptable, be sure to get a copy of its letter for your files. The ethics committees in both the Senate and House are set up to protect members from unethical conduct, as well as to discipline members who violate the rules. In many cases, committee counsel can provide the member and you with proper clearance; but it is important that you receive this in writing before you make what could be an embarrassing mistake.

Campaign Contributions

Contributions to congressional campaigns are regulated by a plethora of federal laws. The traditional cash contribution, although still the most common, can take a number of forms, some of which appear to be creatures of the law rather than of common sense. If, for example, an individual is given, in addition to his regular vacation or leave period, a leave of absence from his regular job to work in a congressional campaign, this can be construed as a contribution in kind to the candidate and must be declared in the candidate's report to the Federal Election Commission. Similarly, the use of a meeting hall for a political rally may be regarded as a contribution in kind if the owner of the facility generally charges a fee for rental of that property. If a car rental firm gives a congressman free use of one of its vehicles during his campaign, this might not only be regarded as a contribution in kind, but, also declared a violation of corporate contribution statutes and thus illegal. On the other hand, if a *volunteer* campaign worker uses his own car to transport other volunteers to and from campaign headquarters or to attend political rallies, this would not ordinarily be regarded as a contribution in kind.

Laws governing campaign contributions are almost as complex as the tax statutes and are a minefield for the unwary. If your group decides to make a contribution to a campaign, particularly if it involves anything other than a straight cash contribution, you should first consult with the candidate's campaign treasurer to determine the appropriateness and legality of the gift. You should also insist upon a letter from the campaign treasurer specifying the nature of the gift, that the treasurer has made a determination that such a gift is legal, and that it will be appropriately reported. When it comes to the law concerning campaign contributions, you should not merely trust your good judgment; the law, as almost everyone knows, is not always logical.

Aside from the pitfalls of noncash contributions, you should bear one rule in mind: payments to a candidate of cash or other things of value are almost always illegal unless directly related to campaign financing. Although there are a number of exceptions to this rule, you should try to avoid them. You cannot afford to risk ruining the reputation of your organization or your issue by taking unnecessary chances. Your immutable rule should be that cash gifts over five dollars can be made only to campaign committees, never to a member of Congress or her staff personally. Second, every contribution you make to a campaign committee should be recorded and reported to the appropriate authorities.

The contribution laws are both complex and frustrating, but you can avoid most of the pitfalls if you adopt the following procedures:

1. Never give actual cash (bank notes, coins, stock, or other apparently untraceable monetary instruments). Such contributions may be legal, but they make record keeping difficult and are inherently suspicious. All contributions to a political campaign should be by personal check, a check from a political action committee (PAC), or its equivalent. Corporate checks, partnership checks, labor union checks, and so on should never be used, even though they may be technically legal under certain *very* restricted circumstances.

2. For most organizations, gifts to political campaigns by check present no problem. It is almost always better to give a campaign committee fifty five-dollar checks than one check for two hundred fifty dollars. There are some circumstances, however, when you or your organization may actually have "real" money that you wish to contribute. This can occur if you have a fund-raiser (for example a picnic) and someone passes the hat for the candidate's

campaign. At the end of the day you may wind up with two or three hundred used dollar bills with no indication where they came from. In this situation, *do not* merely ship off the loot to the candidate's campaign committee. A responsible individual should count the money, deposit it in his own checking account, and write a check to the campaign committee for that amount. The check should be sent to the campaign committee with a letter of explanation. A sample might be as follows:

Congressman Lloyd Kreeger
Kreeger for Congress Committee
1416 Pearl Street
Boulder, Colorado

Dear Congressman Kreeger:

Attached is my personal check for $246.00 for your reelection campaign. This sum represents the amount collected at the Flat Earth Society Annual Picnic last week. Jim Barstow passed the hat for you, and almost everyone there chipped in a dollar or two. Everyone in the Boulder County chapter was invited, and I attach a membership list for your files. I deposited the money in my account and the attached check represents the total of all the cash contributions. I hope this procedure is acceptable to your campaign committee. If your campaign treasurer has any questions, please have him or her contact me directly.

As you know, all of us in the Boulder County Flat Earth Society strongly support you.

Sincerely,

Alice Goosebumple
Secretary/Treasurer

Some campaign treasurers are leery of accepting cash even through this indirect method, but at least they have your letter of explanation to clarify their records.

3. Keep accurate records. Federal election law requires that all contributions be accompanied by the donor's name, occupation, and address, as well as his employer's name. Most congressional campaign committees have preprinted contribution cards, but if you do not have access to these, you should be sure to advise all of your members to include this information on a separate piece of paper when they send in their contributions. This saves the congressman the time and expense of having to request it later.

   You should also be diligent about keeping records of the contributions made by members of your group. This is extremely valuable political information that can be used later. Instruct your members, either in one of your regular newsletters or in a special letter, to let you know each time they make a contribution, to whom it was made, and the amount so that you can keep a tally sheet. This is particularly important if your organization has decided to endorse candidates for public office. You need to know how effective your fund-raising efforts have been so that you can claim appropriate credit from the congressman.

   It is also important to keep accurate records of individual contributions for legal reasons. Not only are some contributions tax-deductible, but individuals legally cannot give more than a certain amount to any particular candidate. Since election regulations change frequently, you should ask the treasurer of the campaign committee about currently prevailing laws if you have any doubt about the appropriateness of the contribution.

4. Don't take chances. As noted previously, all sorts of donations to a campaign may be regarded as cash under the law. Both you and the candidate could be embarrassed by unreported or insufficiently documented contributions. Virtually every campaign committee retains legal counsel for advice on prevailing election law. If you have any doubt about whether a donation must be reported or how it should be reported, consult the treasurer of the campaign committee, who may then consult his lawyer. You should request a legal opinion letter *before* making a contribution. This will protect both you and the candidate.

Nonpolitical Contributions

Although you should never give money directly to a member of Congress or her staff, there are many nonpolitical contributions you can make that are not affected by either the Federal Election Campaign Act or any of the ethics rules. These nonpolitical contributions include expenditures for advertising your issue (as opposed to endorsement of candidates) in the media, contributions to nonpolitical groups that share your views, and public interest activities such as "get-out-the-vote" campaigns (so long as you are not acting on behalf of a particular candidate).

Due to the stringency of the election and ethics laws, nonpolitical expenditures have become extremely popular in recent years. Such devices as ranking congressmen according to their voting records on issues relevant to a particular group's cause are generally regarded as nonpolitical, even if such ranking is published at the group's expense in major newspapers. (Remember, this type of activity can get you into trouble unless it is done very carefully. Before you publish your ranking, you should get a legal opinion letter.)

So prevalent have nonpolitical contributions become that some public interest groups have denounced them as de facto loopholes in the campaign laws. They argue that the distinction between political and nonpolitical is so vague that the law should be expanded to cover so-called nonpolitical contributions. The danger in enacting a truly comprehensive statute to prohibit or regulate such expenditures is obvious. The First Amendment to the Constitution guarantees citizens the right to petition the government. A comprehensive statute would have to regulate even an individual writing to a congressman on his own behalf or flying to Washington to see his senator. Worse yet, an individual taxpayer might be prohibited from taking out an ad in his local newspaper denouncing a property tax increase, or a group might be barred from publicly displaying its views on a billboard. Such restrictions would fly squarely in the face of First Amendment guarantees of freedom of expression and would almost surely be struck down by the courts.

There are also a number of technical loopholes in the Federal Election Campaign Act and in the ethics rules of both the House and Senate. These exceptions are so narrow, however, that you should not attempt to use them unless specifically requested to do so by a member of Congress, and after you have a firm *written* legal opinion from an attorney that such exceptions are appropriate.

The general rule to follow with regard to nonpolitical contributions is that the expenditure of money on promotion of an *issue* rather than a candidate for public office is a right almost universally guaranteed by the Constitution.

Reporting Contributions

The major trap into which many groups fall is not illegal contributions per se, but failing to adequately report what are otherwise permissible gifts. In most cases, contributions to campaign committees will be reported by the committees themselves; you need do nothing more than tell the campaign committee the names, addresses, employers, occupations, and telephone numbers of the donors. If you or any member of your group intends to give more than one thousand dollars to a particular candidate, however, certain additional reporting requirements may be applicable. In this event, be sure to contact the treasurer of the applicable campaign committee for a legal opinion concerning appropriate reporting procedures. *Do not* merely read the Federal Election Campaign Act and decide on your own whether a contribution needs to be reported. That law is reinterpreted so often that you must rely on legal counsel for the most up-to-date regulatory status. This is particularly important with contributions in kind. In certain circumstances, the use of your own office can be regarded as a contribution in kind and must be reported to the federal election authorities. Even if it is subsequently determined that your contribution was legal, you should protect yourself and the candidate you are supporting, *in advance* so that you can preempt any adverse publicity, much less prosecution.

When, How, and How Much to Give to Whom

One of the factors that discourage many groups from making political contributions is the inordinately high cost of campaigns. Today, even minor congressional campaigns cost upward of three hundred thousand dollars. Faced with those kinds of expenditures, many groups wonder whether it is worth contributing at all, given their limited resources. The obvious answer is yes. The question is really to whom.

A group is usually better advised to make twelve one-hundred-dollar contributions than one twelve-hundred-dollar contribution; you should be selective in your list of recipients. It is not necessary for you or your group to give five thousand dollars to a particular candidate in order to be noticed. On the other hand, an organization might be regarded as downright miserly if it could only afford five dollars for a particular candidate's reelection campaign. This rule does not apply to individuals: their five-dollar contributions are welcome by most campaigns as demonstrating solid grassroots support. In general, organization contributions in the one-hundred to five-hundred-dollar range are most appropriate.

Your first step in determining whom your group will support will be to analyze the state of your finances. If you have only two hundred dollars, you should concentrate on two or, at most, three candidates. As your finances improve, you gain more flexibility in the number of people you can support. In this regard, establishment of a political action committee (PAC) may be desirable. These committees are provided for in the Federal Election Campaign Act and allow you to aggregate the individual contributions of your members. This in turn gives you much better control of where your group's contributions are going and concentrates your political influence. There are currently hundreds of PACs, ranging from corporations to special interest groups. They are easy and inexpensive to set up, but you should have an attorney assist you with their establishment. This should cost very little (usually in the three-hundred to five-hundred-dollar range). The Federal Election Commission will also send you, for free, information on the establishment and operation of PACs.

After you have determined the number of campaign contributions your group can make, your second priority should be to decide who the recipients will be. In general, it is a good rule to stand by your friends. Thus, you should give the highest priority to congressmen who have not only voted on your side of your issue, but who have actively assisted in promoting your cause. If there are a number of equally deserving candidates, you should give to the ones with whom you have the strongest constituent ties. If you have any money left after making these contributions, give to incumbent members of Congress who have supported your position.

Finally, if you still have some money to spare, consider gifts to challengers of your strongest opponents. It is extremely unwise, however, to merely attempt to defeat your opponents without first determining what position their replacements would take on your issue. Before you make a contribution to any challengers, be sure you have their support on your position. It is also much more important to retain your friends than to attempt to defeat enemies, particularly given the limited resources of most grassroots lobbying campaigns.

You should *never* contribute to both candidates in a campaign in the hope of currying favor with whoever wins. Since campaign contributions are a matter of public record, most candidates will check their opponent's contributors. You will not fool anybody if you try to play both sides of the street; you will merely squander your resources.

However limited your contribution funds, you can maximize the effectiveness of your contributions through proper timing. Most contributors wait until the polls show a clear leader in an election before they spend their money. Congressmen know this, and although even late dollars are appreciated, early money is the most desirable. You are almost always better off making your decision early in an election year and contributing at least half your total gifts before the primary elections. Since so few people contribute early, congressmen who read the lists are likely to remember your name. Thus you will make more of an impression.

Raising Money

Fund-raising is one of the most complex aspects of politics both from a legal and a practical point of view. Before you raise money for any particular candidate (if you don't have a PAC), you should seek explicit *written* advice from the treasurer of the candidate's campaign committee regarding what you are legally permitted to do. Most campaign committees prefer that you establish a PAC and then donate the money directly to them rather than act as a surrogate fund-raiser for the committee itself. If you decide on the latter, be sure to be familiar with all legal aspects.

If you take the safer and more effective approach of forming a political action committee, you can ask your members for contributions not to candidates, but to the PAC itself. A sample fund-raising letter might read as follows:

Dear Fellow Flat Earth Believer:

Did you know that legislation that would virtually abolish flat earthism as a matter of federal law is currently pending in the Congress? Did you know that this legislation already has fifty cosponsors? Did you know that your tax dollars will be used to attack your beliefs?

Most of you are aware of these facts but don't know what to do. The best way to stop spending your tax dollars to kill your own beliefs is to invest in those who truly represent your feelings. Today, dozens of flat earth congressmen have been targeted by round earthers who want to abolish flat earthism with your own money. We simply must stop them.

The round earthers are putting together "war chests" totaling hundreds of thousands of dollars to deny you representation in the Congress. You could, of course, contribute to one or two congressmen or senators who share your views; but if you are like most of us, you don't have the means to match the big money of round earthers. There is one alternative: by combining hundreds of small five-dollar and ten-dollar contributions, the Flat Earth Political Action Committee (FLATPAC) can concentrate its resources on the key campaigns to save our friends on Capitol Hill from the round earth attack.

Together we can concentrate our resources on the really critical races to make sure our voice is heard. FLATPAC is composed of people just like you and me who are concerned about the direction our country is taking and want to preserve flat earthism as a fundamental right of belief.

Won't you please help us today by enclosing your contribution of five, ten, twenty-five, or fifty dollars? The future of flat earthism depends on you.

Sincerely,

Bret Collins, Chairman
FLATPAC

In addition to such fund-raising letters, your PAC should use every other means of reaching potential contributors. Some PACs retain outside consultants to assist them in mass-mailing efforts. If you decide to do this, you should get a very good idea of cost before signing a contract. Many of these fund-raising efforts require phenomenal amounts of money, in addition to the consultant's fee, and return only a few cents on every dollar they collect in contributions. Administrative and mailing costs can gobble up most of your intended contributions unless you maintain very tight control. Be particularly leery of promoters who promise to raise millions of dollars. The question is not how much they raise, but how much they keep. After expenses, a well-managed campaign that raises one hundred thousand dollars may keep eighty thousand. Another campaign may raise two hundred fifty thousand, but nets only forty thousand. This is not to suggest that mass-mailing campaigns are not useful, if only to put your name in front of the public; but they are not a panacea for empty PAC coffers.

Keeping Accounts

If you decide to raise money either through a PAC, individually, or with a professional fund-raising agency, you must be sure to maintain accurate records. You should keep a written record of every dollar that comes in, including the name, address, employer, occupation, and telephone number of each contributor, and where the money is *spent*.

The Federal Election Commission has a number of statutory as well as regulatory requirements for record keeping, but these are only a start. Set up books according to accepted accounting principles. Not only is this a good business practice, but it will enable you to comply with reporting rules that may not be devised yet. The more thoroughly you are able to document your expenditures, the less concern you need have about compliance with the Federal Election Campaign Act and other applicable statutes. Dealing with money is one of the most complex areas of lobbying. Even if you don't like lawyers, you should talk to them early in your efforts. It is cheaper to talk to your lawyer now than their lawyer later.

The Fund Raiser

Once you have decided to contribute to a particular member or challenger, you should attempt to get the most for your dollar.

Most congressional campaigns raise the bulk of their money through fund-raisers. Usually these are receptions held in Washington or the home district to which lobbyists are given one free ticket for each contribution (often in the one- to two-hundred-dollar range). For that kind of money, you might expect at least some pretty good food; don't bet on it. The purpose of the fund-raiser is just that. Every cent spent on cold shrimp comes right out of the campaign coffers.

How to Be Invited

If you have one hundred dollars to spend, it is easy to be invited to a fund-raiser. Merely call the congressional office concerned and ask to be added to the "contribution list." You will certainly be invited to the next reception.

When the invitation arrives, it is invariably impressive. Usually it will appear to be a request from other congressmen (generally ranking members of the candidate's party) that you attend a reception in the candidate's honor. Don't believe it. The reception is being held by the candidate's campaign committee. The "hosts" will make a token appearance and leave after about five minutes.

How to Accept an Invitation

The invitation will include an RSVP card and a return envelope. The RSVP card is not merely a courtesy. It will request your name, address, occupation, employer, and telephone number(s). This information is required by the Federal Election Campaign Act and will be reported to the Federal Election Commission. Fill it out, but do not return it in the envelope provided. That envelope will be addressed to the candidate's campaign headquarters, not her congressional office. It may never be seen by the candidate or her regular staff if you don't send it to them. But don't just drop it in the mail. Write a letter, attaching the RSVP card and your check. The letter should be very informal and should not mention issues. Such a letter might be as follows:

Dear Congresswoman Kate Lumpen,

Enclosed is a small contribution for your campaign. All of us in the Flat Earth Society are pulling for you.

I'm looking forward to seeing you on the nineteenth.

Sincerely,

Suzie Smith
Member, Flat Earth Society

The candidate's regular staff will send your RSVP card to the campaign committee (to which the original return envelope was addressed), but since there is money attached, there is a good chance they will read your letter. By following this procedure, you have put your name—and the name of your group—before the people who count.

In making your contribution, *make sure to:*

1. Make your check out to the campaign committee indicated on the invitation or solicitation letter, *not* to the candidate personally.

2. Mark the check and your checkbook roster with the candidate's name for your records.

3. Use only personal checks. Corporate, union, or association checks are almost always suspect. *Never* give cash, money orders, or apparently untraceable documents. They look suspicious and can cause considerable embarrassment either to you or the candidate.

Arriving at the Fund-Raiser

Your check is in the mail. You arrive at the reception. The first thing you encounter is a table with staffers behind it. Give them your name; they will check you off the master list of persons from whom they have received contributions. If you have sent your money but your name is not on the list, or if they have no record of having received your contribution, you can save yourself a lot of embarrassment by writing another check on the spot and making a stop payment request on the first check with your bank the next day. Be sure to tell the staffer at the door that is what you intend to do and wait to see that he makes a note of it so he won't be surprised when the first check shows up. Given the efficiency of the mails and some congressional staffs, delays in receiving (or recording) your contribution are fairly common, particularly if you send the check to the regular congressional staff as suggested above.

At most receptions, guests will be given name tags. Put yours on your right side (it's easier to read when shaking hands with someone).

There will usually be a reception line with the candidate, his or her spouse, a staffer, and perhaps even one of the hosts. Don't expect Amy Vanderbilt protocol at one of these receptions. This is politics, not a debutante ball. Be brief in the receiving line. Remind the candidate and his staffer of your name and organization. You'll get a few minutes to chat with the candidate later in the reception if you're aggressive enough.

Liquor and Food

Head for the food or the bar, according to your own preference. A word about drinking: although the liquor is free at fund-raisers, the serious lobbyist should realize that his is not a social event in the usual sense of the term. It is a business function. You'll be discussing serious issues, and that becomes difficult if you've had too much to drink. Your reputation and that of your issue may well be judged by your actions, and people aren't inclined to take drunks seriously. Have one or, at the most, two small drinks. If you aren't comfortable unless you have something that looks strong in your hand, order a Virgin Mary, a tonic on the rocks, or a lime and Coke. People don't drink milk at fund-raisers unless they are trying to impress a Wisconsin congressman.

Don't expect to satisfy a ravenous hunger at a fund-raiser. Usually the fare will consist of canapés and other hors d'oeuvres. Have one or two and reserve a table at a nearby restaurant for later.

Circulating

Most of the other people at the fund-raiser will be lobbyists, too. All, or almost all, will be friendly, harassed, tired, and slightly egotistical; but they can be a gold mine of information. They are easy to meet at receptions such as this and, despite some huddles in the corners, they enjoy circulating. Meet as many as possible by asking what problems they are working on. Usually they'll be more than happy to tell you.

During the reception, watch for the breakup of the receiving line; that signals that the candidate is going to circulate. Position yourself in a convenient place, and politely but firmly see to it that you get the candidate's attention.

Always start out by thanking the candidate for inviting you, and remind him of your group. Next, tell him how much you appreciate his support on your issue (even if he has waffled on it from time to time). Finally, tell him you intend to go back to your group and encourage all of them to support him (there are ten thousand ways to do this). Get the above points in your conversation, but don't state it as crazily as I have.

Be sure to give the candidate one of your business cards (see page 111). Also give a card to his staffer. The cards will eventually find their way into the candidate's cross index files if his staff is at all efficient.

Don't discuss the detailed points of your issue with the candidate at the fund-raiser unless she asks you a specific question. Detailed discussions are much more appropriate—and more useful—in her office. Before you leave her, ask her or her staffer for an appointment, unless you just saw her that week. She will undoubtedly agree, but will be vague on timing. Tell her you are tentatively free about three days hence, and that you will call her secretary to confirm. Be sure her staffer is made aware of this. You will go to the staffer—not the candidate—if her personal secretary is reluctant to arrange the meeting when you call.

Most fund-raisers are in the late afternoon or early evening, and are generally held on Tuesday, Wednesday, or Thursday. It is considered somewhat bad form to be among the last to leave the party, so you should plan on staying about an hour or so—not until the bar closes. Often you'll find other lobbyists or staffers with interests similar to yours at these functions. If you feel up to it, invite them for a light dinner. Meeting other lobbyists builds your network of contacts, an invaluable resource.

Following up

The next day, follow up:

1. Write to the congressman or candidate, again reminding him of your issue. One form is as follows:

Dear Congressman Jesse Keelover:

I enjoyed seeing you last night. As you know, the Flat Earth Society has always appreciated your support, and we are particularly grateful for your help in turning back H.R. 506. There have been several recent developments with regard to that bill that I would like to discuss with you at your convenience.

Thank you again for your help.

Sincerely,

Don Jones

2. Write—or better yet, call—the staffers you met at the reception. Remind them of the appointment you set up with the member, and ask them to arrange a convenient time for the meeting. Stress

that you would like to see them first, and follow the procedures outlined in Chapter 11.

3. Write a short, polite note to all the other people you met at the fund-raiser. It's only for their files, and to reestablish yourself in their memory. Keep a careful record of the fund-raisers you have attended, just as you do for other political contributions. This will be useful in the future. One trick is to mark every business card you receive with the date and circumstances of your meeting. Have this information recorded on your Rolodex.

Fund-raisers are generally regarded as a necessary evil by candidates. These events expose them to all sorts of people they would rather not see, but it's not easy to refuse to talk to someone who has spent one hundred dollars for five minutes. The lobbyists should use that five minutes—or even one minute—to the greatest advantage. Candidates love contributors who are neither seen nor heard from, but you must be both.

Fourteen

★ ★ ★ ★ ★

Gimmicks

★ ★ ★ ★ ★

You can fool too many of the people too much of the time.
—James Thereby

Given the hundreds of special interest groups in Washington, it is sometimes difficult to be noticed. This is particularly true of smaller organizations. Sometimes a citizen lobby resorts to unconventional methods merely to get some attention from the press or some public notoriety. Reasoned, temperate debate neither sells newspapers nor attracts viewers to the six o'clock news. For this reason, gimmicks may be one of the only ways to spark the media interest you feel you deserve. If you go this route, however, you should be sure the stunt you choose does not detract from your basic objective. The medium, in other words, cannot overwhelm the message. Before you resort to a gimmick to promote your cause, consider the following factors.

Keep It Relevant to Your Issue

Mere grandstanding will not convey the message you want, however clever your stunt. One of the best recent gimmicks was staged by the right-to-life forces who deluged Capitol Hill with thousands of roses, each symbolizing an aborted fetus. This was both dramatic and relevant to the issue. Whoever thought of it was a media genius.

Don't Be Disruptive

Although the American Agriculture Movement's "tractorcade" to Washington was certainly relevant to its issue (low commodity prices), the disruption caused by hundreds of tractors destroying the mall angered so many people that the farmers probably defeated their own purpose. A peaceful, even humorous, gimmick is much more likely to be favorably covered by the media.

Be Visible

Gimmicks sent through the mail rarely attract the kind of publicity you want, although they may get some attention on Capitol Hill. Your gimmick is basically a publicity stunt and must be visual to be picked up on the evening news. For example, mere complaints about rats in public housing projects are rarely enough to attract the broadcast media; but a full cage of rats mounted on the top of a station wagon and driven down Pennsylvania Avenue might dramatize the issue. (A few years ago, this stunt was successfully attempted in Washington. Some would suggest, however, that the promoters went a little far in threatening to let loose thousands of rats in federal offices and residential areas if their demands were not acceded to.)

Contact the Press

No matter how clever, how relevant to your cause, or how visible, your gimmick will do you little good unless it is actually picked up by the media. Before you stage any stunt, be sure to alert the local media, particularly the television and radio stations. In Washington you should contact the news directors of the following major U.S. stations:

WETA–TV Channel 26
P.O. Box 2626
Washington, D.C. 20013
(703) 998-8100

WJLA–TV Channel 7
3007 Tilden St., N.W.
Washington, D.C. 20008
(202) 364-7777

WFTY–TV Channel 50
2121 Wisconsin Ave., N.W.
Washington, D.C. 20007
(202) 965-5050

WRC–TV Channel 4
4001 Nebraska Ave., N.W.
Washington, D.C. 20016
(202) 885-4083

WTTG–TV Channel 5
5151 Wisconsin Ave., N.W.
Washington, D.C. 20016
(202) 244-5151

WNVT–TV Channel 53
8101–A Lee Highway
Falls Church, VA 22042
(703) 698-9682

WUSA–TV Channel 9
4100 Wisconsin Ave., N.W.
Washington, D.C. 20016
(202) 895-5999

Keep It Cheap

Your gimmick is more likely to be effective if you stress grassroots participation than if you go the route of costly extravaganzas. Use your imagination instead of your checkbook.

Although you must gear your gimmick to your particular issue, the following are a few examples of successful gimmicks used over the past few years that conform to the rules outlined above.

For years, the National Broiler Council staged a "chicken dog feast" in the courtyards of the Senate and House office buildings to acquaint the Senate and House staffs with chicken-meat hot dogs. The issue being promoted by the National Broiler Council (the chicken producers) was that chicken dogs tasted similar, if not identical, to regular beef or pork hot dogs and that they should not be required to label their product "artificial hot dogs." These chicken dog feasts were usually held at about five o'clock on Friday afternoons during the summertime and included beer and potato chips. They were attended by staff members of both the House and Senate. The drawing card was not the hot dogs themselves, but the free beer that accompanied them. Nevertheless, the chicken dog issue became a cause célèbre, and the National Broiler Council ultimately was successful. The total cost of chicken dog feasts probably did not exceed a few thousand dollars per year, but they were known throughout Washington as one of the most ingenious and successful lobbying campaigns in recent memory.

Each year the Can Manufacturers Institute distributes beautiful Christmas tree ornaments fashioned from cleverly reshaped tin cans. Although CMI is not attempting to promote a specific bill, everyone in Washington recognizes the CMI ornaments and remembers them at least for one month a year.

The Distilled Spirits Council (DISCUS) not only sends samples of its products around the Hill at various times of the year, but also provides congressional offices with posters and other advertising material to distribute to members' constituencies urging responsibility in alcohol use. The members, in turn, can send these to high schools in their districts for incalculable political benefits—all at little cost to DISCUS.

The electric utilities have distributed free light bulbs to the Hill. Although the total cost of this project was probably significant, the lobby certainly did not violate any gift restrictions since each recipient received only one or two.

Various conservation groups have visited the Hill with enormous displays of leg-hold traps to publicize their view that such devices are cruel to animals. The displays were widely covered by the media and resulted in federal legislation restricting the use of such devices.

The Ferrous Scrap Consumers Coalition distributed to the Hill paperweights made of steel scrap and emblazoned with the message that this commodity was one of America's vanishing resources. Thousands were given away at a nominal cost to the steel companies.

A fifty-five-gallon drum of polluted river water was brought to Washington by an environmentalist group that threatened to dump it in the Potomac as a media stunt if stricter water pollution control guidelines were not adopted. It is not known what happened to the polluted water, but the desired environmental legislation was adopted.

These are only some of the ideas others have come up with to publicize their programs. Undoubtedly you can think of even more effective stunts.

Fifteen

★ ★ ★ ★ ★

The Hill Blitz

★ ★ ★ ★ ★

A politician will double cross that bridge if he comes to it.
—Oscar Levant

What Is a Blitz?

The most formidable short-term pressure you can put on your congressional delegation and the most efficient means of consolidating your resources is the blitz. As the name implies, a "blitz" is the swift movement of all of your resources to Congressional offices. These resources are primarily people, and coordinating them demands the generalship of a Rommel. It is a concentrated and effective means of expressing your views on Capitol Hill and should be included in every lobbying campaign.

In the last decade, the Hill blitz has approached an art form. In this kind of strategic two- to three-day attack on Capitol Hill, you will have to use all available resources, including constituent contacts and favors owed from congressional offices. Although a blitz entails an incredible amount of logistical work, it is the best use of these debts and your power.

The major challenge of a Hill blitz is not substantive but procedural. To be successful, a Hill blitz must be planned weeks or even months in advance; you must have the most senior representatives of your cause in Washington at the same time. The effectiveness of a blitz—for both your members and the Hill—becomes attenuated if you spread it out over a week or two. The blitz can be a frustrating experience, and your own presence of mind will be severely tried during its planning stage.

Preparation and Appointments

As a rule, you should count on at least three weeks to adequately prepare even a modest blitz. The more members you have coming to town, the more time you should allow yourself. As with demonstrations, the logistics of a Hill blitz are much more time-consuming than the actual lobbying. Your administrative concerns will be identical in most respects to those involved in planning a demonstration (see Chapter 7).

The distinction between a demonstration (a loose amalgam of people chanting in the streets) and a blitz is your focus on the Hill. Before you make a single telephone call to arrange an appointment, you must prepare a thorough analysis of crucial congressmen, cross-indexed with your blitz participants on the basis of constituent relations, interest in your issue, committee assignments, and past support. You should have already prepared your list of target members, together with their backgrounds, in the resource book (see Chapters 3 and 4). On most issues, your list will probably not exceed forty-five members of Congress.

The first priority in determining who will visit each of the members is constituent relations. Participants in the blitz from a member's district should always be given precedence in meeting their representative. Try to arrange meetings on this basis by calling the offices of each of the members for whom you will have a constituent participating in the blitz. Tell the appointments secretary the nature of your issue and that a constituent of the member will be in Washington two to three weeks hence. Request a meeting on a particular day, and be sure to get two or three alternative times during the period of the blitz when the member would be able to meet with your people. Tell the appointments secretary that you will call to reconfirm one of the times within a few days. Repeat this process with each of the Hill offices until you have a schedule of available times and people. Obviously, the reason you have requested alternate dates is that your calendar will be filled with conflicts and you want to be able to shift meeting times around.

After you have completed your constituent congressmen calls, contact the congressional offices that have given you the greatest support. Even though it may appear that you are lobbying the converted, you cannot afford to alienate your friends by ignoring them. They should at least be given the courtesy of a visit and be kept informed of your efforts.

Finally, you should contact committee and subcommittee chairmen and all other members of Congress who have a direct impact upon your issue. The actual number of offices you should contact will, of course, depend on the number of participants in your blitz, their constituent relations, and the time your participants are prepared to spend in Washington.

After you have completed all your preliminary calls, you should divide the participants in your blitz into three- or four-person teams. Each team should be assigned to visit not more than six congressional offices in a given day. The reason for this modest number of visits, particularly in view of the fact that most interviews will not take more than fifteen to twenty minutes, is logistical. Even though you will have made appointments, delays are inevitable. Particularly when the Congress is in session, meetings are often interrupted by roll-call votes, committee meetings, telephone calls, and other more urgent appointments. Most congressmen like to think of themselves as being flexible, much to the consternation of anyone attempting to pin them down to a particular time for a meeting. Also, since you will be emphasizing *constituent* contacts, you should permit plenty of time for walking from one congressional office to the next. This is especially true if you have to go from the House to the Senate side to visit the constituent members. You should allow at least fifteen to twenty minutes to get from one office to the next, especially if your blitz participants are unfamiliar with the Hill.

Your constituent blitz participants should be made team leaders, and if possible you should not put all constituents from a member's district on the same team. This way you will be able to have a broader coverage of representation. If there are an inordinately large number of blitz participants from a single state or congressional district, you may want to schedule a joint meeting of several teams with the member. If you do this, be sure to tell the appointments secretary so that accommodations can be made. Most members' offices will accommodate only six or seven people comfortably.

After you have designated your teams, you should schedule them for times when the members are available, placing the highest priority on constituent relations. Then make a master calendar of all teams' appointments, cross-indexed by congressman, team, and time. You, as the coordinator, must know where every team will be at all times.

After you have completed your calendar, call back each of the congressional offices and confirm your appointments. Inevitably, between the first time you called and the time you confirm the appointments, there will have been changes in the member's calendar. You will have to rework your schedule several times before it is complete. Even with a modest-sized list, you will have to make scores of telephone calls before you can put your calendar in final form. You should be sure to allow plenty of time to do this; a blitz can't be set up at the eleventh hour. After you have completed your schedule, you should prepare separate calendars for each team. A sample calendar for a team might be as follows:

Flat Earth Society—Congressional Contact Team Number Five

Mary Butrum, Team Leader, Lancaster, PA

David Hawkins, Redlands, CA

Sara Knowles, Fairfield, CT

Monday, 24 September

8:00 a.m., breakfast meeting
All team members at Washington Hilton Hotel

9:30 a.m., depart for Capitol Hill

10:00 a.m., Congresswoman Helen Blanchard (D—PA)
3240 Rayburn House Office Building
Telephone: 555-4613
Staff Contact: Millie Tightfist

10:45 a.m., Congressman James Crossman (R—CA)
320 Cannon House Office Building
Telephone: 555-1716
Staff Contact: Melvin Scrumpus

11:20 a.m., Congressman Lupis Wolf (D—CT)
3270 Rayburn House Office Building
Telephone: 555-7304
Staff Contact: Bill Weevel

12:10 p.m., lunch with staff of Education Subcommittee
(Lorna Doone, Betty Crocker, Frank Bertolli)
209 1/2 Restaurant
209 1/2 Pennsylvania Ave., S.E.
Reservations in name of Mary Butrum

1:45 p.m., Senator Calvin Hoover (R—PA)
421 Dirksen Senate Office Building
Telephone: 555-4163
Staff Contact: Ronald Kennedy

2:30 p.m., Senator Abraham Arthur (D—PA)
3240 Russell Senate Office Building
Telephone: 555-4340
Staff Contact: George Madison

4:00 p.m., Senator James Grant (R—T)
415 Dirksen Senate Office Building
Telephone: 555-7316
Staff Contact: Roosevelt McKinley

5:30 p.m., cocktail reception for congressmen and staff
Gold Room, Rayburn House Office Building

Tuesday, 25 September

8:00 a.m., breakfast for all team members
Washington Hilton Hotel

9:30 a.m., depart for Capitol Hill

10:15 a.m., Congressman J. D. "Whimpie" Burke (D—CA)
1421 Longworth House Office Building
Telephone: 555-2166
Staff Contact: Benjamin Dover

11:00 a.m., Congresswoman Stella Schnellzug (R—CT)
3160 Longworth House Office Building
Telephone: 555-2146
Staff Contact: Harry David

*12:15 p.m., lunch with members of Senate Education Committee
(Plato Brown, Mauna Lowa)*
The Man in the Green Hat Restaurant
301 Massachusetts Ave., N.E.
Reservations in name of Mary Butrum

2:00 p.m., depart National Airport

All team members, as well as the team captain, will be given a copy of the schedule, along with the following items:

1. short biographies of each member of Congress with whom they have an appointment
2. summary sheets to leave with each congressional office
3. interview sheets

The interview sheets are to be filled out by the team member after each congressional visit. They describe in detail the nature of the meeting and any commitments made by the congressman to the group. Also included should be the personal reactions of each team member to the interview—whether it went smoothly, whether the congressman was hostile or friendly, whether he seemed to be aware of the issue. Finally, each team member should indicate what questions were asked by the congressman or his staff members. You will follow up on these later.

Coordination

In addition to making all the appointments on the Hill, developing a comprehensive calendar of meetings and hundreds of other logistical problems, you must be sure the lines of authority for managing the blitz are clearly demarcated. It would be an unusual group that did not have five or six individuals who are impossible to satisfy with regard to their schedules and who will want to depart from their assigned interviews. There has never been a Hill blitz in which something did not go wrong—appointments canceled, participants lost, meetings missed, or congressmen insulted. During the blitz, your place is not on Capitol Hill, but in a central location with a telephone. If possible, you should have an aide assigned to making spot checks on the Hill to see that everything is going as planned. There will, however, be dozens of questions posed both by your team members and congressional staffers; you must be reachable quickly.

When two or more organizations are participating in the Hill blitz, coordination among the various groups is essential. It is generally best not to include members of different groups on the same teams unless you have a very close and long-standing working relationship. Mixing team members is an invitation to personal and institutional rivalries that can detract from your message. You should, however, have a single coordinator for the entire blitz agreed upon in advance by all participating groups. You cannot afford to have six different sets of instructions for your group. As coordinator, you will also be responsible for making luncheon plans and in some cases dinner reservations for teams meeting with congressmen, restructuring team membership as required by unforeseen events, and following up any questions raised by Hill staff or members. The role of coordinator in a Hill blitz is time-consuming and difficult, but it is also critical to a successful effort.

The Meeting

The actual meetings of your members with their senators and congressmen should follow the procedures outlined in Chapter 11. During a blitz, however, you will not be present at the actual interviews. It is therefore important that the team captains be fully briefed on your entire lobbying campaign. In this regard, it is desirable to have the team captains meet separately with you just prior to the blitz. At this meeting, you will describe the logistics of the blitz, procedures to be followed in the congressional meetings, and the strategy and tactics of your lobbying campaign. Team leaders should be provided with a resource book (see Chapter 3). As noted previously, this book should be held in confidence and should not be distributed to all team members. The team leaders, however, should be given an opportunity to thoroughly familiarize themselves with the issues, statistics, and facts before they are unleashed on the Hill. It will be the team leader's responsibility to be sure all appointments are kept, protocol is observed, and facts are presented in the way you intend. The team leaders will act as your surrogate at the meetings; you cannot afford to let them go ill prepared. Be sure to review with them the procedures outlined in Chapter 11, and try to answer all questions before they arise on the Hill. Also emphasize to the team leaders the importance of maintaining a schedule and limiting their interviews with congress-men to fifteen or twenty minutes. Finally, stress the importance of filling out the interview sheets. It will be the team leader's responsi-bility to collect these and give them to you following the blitz.

Several trade associations train team leaders by staging congres-sional meetings that dramatize the methodology to be employed. This is an extremely effective method of training your troops and should be done not more than twenty-four hours in advance of your actual blitz.

Follow-Up

Perhaps the most important part of your Hill blitz is following up on the contacts you have made. The first step in this procedure is to review all the interview sheets prepared by your team members. First priority should go to answering questions posed by members of Con-gress or their staffs. If the nature of the question implies a degree of urgency (such as how your organization stands on a bill pending on the floor of the House), you should follow up with a telephone call to the appropriate staff member of the congressman asking the ques-tion.

In most cases, questions will not be so urgent as to demand tele-phone follow-up. They should, however, be promptly answered in writing. If you receive too many obvious questions, it may be an indi-cation that your team leader has not been fully briefed; you should review the first day's interview sheets immediately so that teams will be able to answer these questions on the spot and you will not have to follow up later. It is always most effective if it appears that your ad-herents are knowledgeable and they don't have to go back to headquarters for answers to the simplest questions.

You should also write to every congressman, senator, and staff member who attended the meetings, thanking them for their cour-tesy in receiving your delegation. This can be a form letter, but you should personalize it if you know the congressman, senator, or staff member involved, or if the staff member was instrumental in assist-ing you to arrange the meeting.

Finally, you should have each team member write personal letters to all the individuals they met during the blitz. These letters should be written within one week after the blitz, and you should request that copies of them be sent to you for your cross-reference files.

Completion of the Blitz

You should be able to make a relatively accurate estimate of your supporters and to analyze your chances of success. Add this information to your resource book, particularly if members of Congress have made commitments to your team regarding their opposition, support, or neutrality on your issue.

Sixteen

★ ★ ★ ★ ★

What If Things Go Wrong?

★ ★ ★ ★ ★

Nothing is so admirable in politics as a short memory.
—John Kenneth Galbraith

In even the most carefully prepared lobbying campaign, many things will go wrong. Appointments will be missed, decimal points dropped in your statistical tables, key congressmen inadvertently left off invitation lists, or an important staffer insulted. Since these slip-ups are virtually inevitable, it is best to prepare for them before they occur.

Errors of Fact

Nothing is more valuable to a lobbyist than his credibility. Congressmen and their staffs know you are expressing a point of view and take that into consideration in making their decision as to how they will act on your issue. They have a right to expect, however, that the objective information (such as statistics, names, dates) that you supply will be complete and accurate. This is particularly important for congressional offices that support your position. If your allies rely upon inaccurate information you have supplied them, there may be embarrassing and even devastating repercussions. This is not to say you shouldn't emphasize facts that enhance your position; but withholding essential information or inventing numbers must be absolutely forbidden.

Additional Information

During the course of any lobbying effort, you will certainly be asked to provide additional information. There is a difference, however, between withholding information and simply not having it available. If you are asked to provide additional information by a congressional office, promise to do so as soon as possible.

Sources

Aside from the ethics of supplying correct information, there is the practical side of fact checking. Time is well spent in proofreading every document you send to the Hill for typographical errors and misstatements of fact. It is also useful if you can supply footnotes or otherwise indicate the source of your information on all documents sent to the Hill. The most credible sources are government agency reports. Information and numbers supplied by your own group are sometimes regarded as being tainted by self-interest. In presenting factual data to congressional offices, it is always best to qualify the information with footnotes or explanations if you have any reason to believe that it may not present the entire picture or may give an incorrect impression.

Statistics

Statistics can be twisted in remarkable ways to demonstrate your point of view. It is important, however, to indicate to the congressional offices the methodology you used to arrive at your statistical base. For example, very small increases of a given number over a period of months or years might represent significant percentage increases. Conversely, a large base number in a given year might not result in significant percentage increases, and the actual numbers should be used. Consider the following charts:

Chart 1

Instances of Ships Falling Off the Edge of the World

1991	13
1992	15
1993	20
1994	25
1995	30
1996	35

(Source: *Flat Earth Society Digest*)

Chart 2

Unexplained Losses of Ships

1991	250
1992	265
1993	271
1994	282
1995	286
1996	291

(Source: *Lloyds of Boston*)

The increase shown in Chart 1 is over 169 percent, but in Chart 2 it is only 16 percent. In presenting your statistics, you will use the percentage figure from Chart 1 and the actual numbers from Chart 2. These methods are not misstatements of fact, but merely examples of how to present your case in the best possible light. You should be very careful to explain this methodology when submitting your statistics. There are much more sophisticated methods of presenting statistics, including use of semilog tables, econometric modeling, and least-square trend lines. You should experiment with various methods to find the one best suited to enhancing your position.

If, no matter how you twist and bend them, the statistics simply do not support your position, resist the temptation to invent numbers or somehow make your numbers serve your purposes. Any attempt to do so will almost always be counterproductive. Remember, your opponents—if they're any good at all—will be scrutinizing your propaganda. If they discover an obvious distortion, the credibility of your entire position will be jeopardized. It's even worse when it appears that you have consciously attempted to deceive members of Congress and their staffs. Your personal trustworthiness and that of your group is at stake. Don't undermine it.

Things Go Wrong

You've decided to play it straight. You've reviewed the numbers and stressed those that most enhance your position. You've double-checked them for errors. Nothing can go wrong, but the typewriter gremlins have it in for you this week and all the decimal points in your statistics have been moved one figure to the left. Documents have already been sent to 117 congressional offices; and speechwriters, relying on the data you supplied, are cranking out blistering commentary on your behalf. Now you discover the error.

The first thing to do when you discover an error is to immediately reproof the entire document. Other mistakes may have crept in, and it is best to correct all errors at one time. Once you are satisfied that all errors have been caught, make a prioritized list of persons who should know about it. If you are aware of certain congressional offices that are preparing speeches, newsletters, or any other documents, *call*—don't write. In most cases the person to contact will be the legislative assistant whose assignment covers your subject matter. Tell the LA of the error or errors and supply the correct information. Also tell her that you will be sending an errata sheet with correct information immediately.

Next pull out your list of recipients of the incorrect information and send them all an errata sheet. If possible the errata sheet should be identical to the page where the errors appeared in the original document. It can be a photocopy of the page with the correct numbers on it. If this is not possible because of the format of the original document, a small paper slip should be sent with the correct information. The errata slip or sheet should be accompanied by a short, straightforward note. The format might be as follows:

Errata

The Flat Earth Society Publication Square Corners, *dated July 8, 1996, contained an error on page 26. A new page 26 with the correct information is attached. Please discard the original page 26 and insert the attached.*

The Flat Earth Society regrets the error.

The important thing about correcting errors is that you do it promptly and that you supply accurate information at the time you make the correction. Correcting simple errors of fact should almost always be done; but don't make a big deal of it. You should flag such errors with the degree of urgency warranted by the nature of the mistake. Typographical errors may be ignored if they do not change the meaning of your statements, but statistical errors should be corrected as soon as possible.

A more difficult situation is an oral or written misstatement of fact by a member of your group to a congressional or administrative office. Often you will not discover such misstatements until days or even weeks have passed. When you realize what has happened, immediately get in touch with the person who conveyed the misinformation. Discuss the matter with him and have him contact the persons to whom he communicated the incorrect information. It is embarrassing for him to have to do this, but the damage will be far greater if you are forced to publicly contradict your own members. If for any reason he refuses, or is unable to correct the error, you should do so yourself in as low-key a manner as possible. *Do not* merely let the matter rest. The most important thing you have going for you is credibility; you cannot allow obvious errors to go uncorrected.

Perhaps the most difficult and sensitive situation of all is when a congressman supporting your position misstates essential facts. This is not a rare occurrence. The *Congressional Record* is replete with errors. These errors can be used both offensively and defensively. You should carefully review all public statements of your opponents and, when you discover an error, use it to your advantage. The best way to do this is to photocopy the offending document, underline the erroneous statements or statistics in red and prepare a short rebuttal piece with accurate statistics. It helps if your rejoinder can be footnoted with unimpeachable sources. The rebuttal piece should then be distributed to all of your allies and, if possible, inserted in the *Congressional Record*. This technique is most useful where major errors of fact are apparent. Do not do this if it makes you appear a nitpicker.

When your own side makes an error, it is generally best to approach the legislative assistant first. You should do this as soon as you discover the error and, you hope, before the other side has noticed it. You should follow the legislative assistant's advice on correcting the misstatement. Some congressional offices will put a correction in the "Extension of Remarks" of the *Congressional Record* immediately; others might choose to explain the discrepancy away through deft use of polemics; and still others might ignore it altogether. Even if they choose the latter course, it is important that you at least notify the congressional office of the mistake. It is unlikely they will repeat the error. If they do, you might consider going to the administrative assistant. These types of errors reflect poorly on the congressman's credibility, and *that* is a political question.

Changed Circumstances

During the course of any lobbying campaign, numbers, names, and even the facts themselves will change. What may have appeared at one point to be an enormous threat to your position may have changed significantly during the course of a bill's pendency in Congress. Change is inevitable, and everyone in Washington recognizes that statistics and other factual bases for your claims become less—or more—reliable as time goes on. About the only way to really go wrong, given the dynamics of the Washington system, is to fail to acknowledge the ephemeral nature of your facts. No one will raise an eyebrow if you change numbers based upon better, more recent information. You will arouse more suspicion by *not* updating your facts. These changes, however, can as often work against you as for you. For example, if you're dealing with a situation in which monthly statistics are a major factor, aberrations in the marketplace can destroy your best arguments almost overnight. As discussed previously, there are ways to update your statistics that, although still accurate, will present a better slant on your position. Consider the following:

Number of Flat Earth Society Members

1992	200
1993	300
1994	650
1995	1,400
1996	912

The above chart shows a decline in the membership of your organization in the most recent year, and this is likely to raise eyebrows on Capitol Hill. One way to handle this problem is to eliminate the chart entirely and include references to membership in the text of your paper. A reworking of the information included in the chart might read as follows: "The Flat Earth Society continues to grow at a remarkable pace. In 1992 it had only 200 members. By 1996, membership stood at 912—an increase of over 400 percent." This technique obviously fails to mention that there was an actual decline in 1996; but it does not raise the suspicion that you have not updated your numbers. This is about as close as you should ever come to a "reworking" of information. But remember, you should be assiduous in keeping your facts and figures current. If you don't, you can be sure your opposition will.

Insults and Breaches of Protocol

Although Washington is often portrayed as a city of impassioned rhetoric, more pointed insults are probably traded on loading docks in Brooklyn than in the U.S. Senate. The Senate is the lair of wordsmiths. Insults are carefully crafted and tenderly slipped between opponents' ribs, sometimes without their knowledge.

Senator Everett Dirksen was fond of retelling the following story about insults on Capitol Hill. "If one of your opponents starts out a speech on the floor by saying, 'My colleague, the senator from Illinois, is mistaken,' then you don't have to worry too much. If he starts out his speech with, 'My esteemed colleague, the distinguished senator from the great state of Illinois, the land of Lincoln. . .,' then you'd better not turn your back."

Although it is possible that you will be insulted during the course of a lobbying campaign, it will probably be artfully done. The rules in reacting to this are simple: don't.

It is different, however, when you (or more likely one of your sup-porters or members) insults a congressman or congressional staff member. This usually happens when lobbyists reach their frustration limit with the bureaucracy, particularly when out-of-town lobbyists visit numerous congressional offices and encounter only inertia. Many people in the hustings tend to regard Washington not just as another city, but as a foreign country populated by a peculiar race of drones. It *can* become frustrating after you've visited fifteen congressional offices and have received nothing but polite assurances from bland young men and women that they will "look into it." A typical reaction at the end of a Hill blitz is for one of your members to look at the twenty-three-year-old who holds the destiny of your issue in his hands and to say something like, "You bastard, have you been listening to what I've been telling you? The whole world's falling apart and you're just sitting there like a clam in gumbo."

Hardly a day passes on the Hill when someone doesn't offer to throw a junior legislative assistant out a fifth-floor window of the Rayburn Building. Perhaps that's why Congress needs so many po-licemen (there are three Capitol cops for every member of Congress). Although such an outburst might make you feel a little less frustrated, it's unlikely to do much for your group's image as moderate, thought-ful, and objective. It also doesn't do your cause any good. Screaming matches tend to reflect an image of extremism and can severely injure your chances of success in both the short and long term. Besides, almost no one on Capitol Hill will be impressed or intimidated by threats or curses.

If such an outburst does occur, however, you should immediately separate the curser from the cursee. Politely but firmly suggest to the member of your group that you think there is little more that can be accomplished and declare the interview terminated. In certain situa-tions this may be difficult to do; your colleague probably won't express much goodwill for you at the time. As soon as possible, go back to the congressional office to salve the wounds. Whether or not you should apologize depends on the circumstances and will be discussed later.

A far more common form of insult in Washington is the "bruised ego" syndrome. Congressmen tend to have an inflated sense of their own worth. This condition is highly contagious and usually affects staff members early in their tenure. Whether their fond self-image is justified is of little consequence; it is not your responsibility to inform them of their true worth. Merely recognize the way things are in

Washington and learn how to deal with the situation. Remember, you're not just lobbying for your own personal satisfaction; your goal is to change the course of legislative events in the country. You can't effectively accomplish this if you don't learn to live with the realities of the world.

The most frequent manner in which tender egos are bruised is not by malfeasance, but by nonfeasance. Legislative assistants are often furious if they are ignored or, worse yet, if a lobbyist goes over their head to an administrative assistant or the member of Congress herself. Some congressmen are highly sensitive to being ignored on issues they feel particularly knowledgeable about. Ignoring such people can be almost as bad as insulting them to their face. Even if they can't do you much good, it can certainly do you a lot of harm to leave key people out of your lobbying plans. Including some of these individuals in your campaign will require a great deal more effort on your part, but not including them can be very dangerous. General rules to follow in this regard are:

1. *Always* keep the legislative assistant of the congressional offices you are in contact with informed of your program and any meetings you have had with his superiors.

2. Include press aides in your rounds if any part of your program consists of press releases by the congressman's office or using the congressman's name.

3. Never refer to congressmen or senators by their first name unless you are extremely good friends. Although few of them will directly contradict you if you use their first name, most enjoy being referred to as "Senator" or "Congressman." It is better to be invited to use first names than to be asked to use the honorific.

4. Get a sense of the degree of formality of a congressional office by seeing how the staff members themselves interact. In some offices three-piece suits are worn, and secretaries refer to AAs and LAs as Mr. or Ms. In others, where open-neck shirts and sunglasses predominate, the only thing you'll hear are nicknames. Try to adjust your approach to the formality of the office and be slightly more formal than they are.

5. Never condescend to anyone in a congressional office, no matter how young or inexperienced the person may appear. Entire lobbying campaigns have been blown by the president of a trade

association referring to a secretary as "little girl," or to an African American LA as "you people."

6. Always be sure the chairman of the subcommittee and the chairman of the full committee that is considering your issue are aware of your existence and what you are attempting to do, even if they are likely to oppose you. This is not to suggest that you must include them in the specifics of every action you intend to take; only that chairmen are highly sensitive about knowing what is going on in their own committees. They can be recalcitrant if they are left in the dark about something. It's not necessary for you to speak to the chairman directly, but his or her staff should receive at least a cursory briefing.

7. Be very judicious in criticizing members of congressional staffs to any other Hill staffers. As large as it is, the Hill staff still regards itself as a family. You may be unaware of personal relationships that exist between the person you are speaking to and the person you are criticizing.

Seventeen

★ ★ ★ ★ ★

Do You Need a Professional?

★ ★ ★ ★ ★

Politics is not a science ... but an art.

—Otto von Bismark

What a Professional Lobbyist Can and Can't Do

If you follow the rules of this book, you should, with a little practice, have no difficulty in organizing your own lobbying campaign. Time, however, is an important factor that must be dealt with. A professional can help you cope with time, as well as provide experience. Never hire a professional lobbyist with the expectation that he can carry the ball for you or buy influence. He will only be a spokesman for your cause; you and your members must still provide the clout necessary for him to present a credible case.

In that respect, hiring a lobbyist is somewhat different from retaining a lawyer. You have a right to expect a lawyer to know considerably more than you do about the intricacies of the law and, after you have told her all the facts in your particular case, you should usually trust her judgment on how a legal proceeding should be handled. In other words, you put yourself and your case in her hands. Although this is true to a certain extent with professional lobbyists, you should feel much more comfortable in helping run your own lobbying campaign than you would in advising counsel on how best to present a case in court. Since lobbyists do not necessarily have any specialized training or experience and few college courses are given on how to lobby (no degree has ever been awarded for this profession), it is possible that you will know as much about lobbying as he does. Also, you will almost certainly know more about your particular issue than any lobbyist you retain. It will be up to you to educate him regarding the facts and politics of your issue. What you are buying, if you decide to retain a lobbyist, is time, dedication, experience in general legislative matters, and organizational ability. Remember, you have to supply the clout yourself.

Over the years, dozens of books have been written and hundreds of stories told about Washington miracle workers who, with one telephone call, could turn around the course of legislative events on behalf of a client. Such stones tend to perpetuate the myth of the omniscient lobbyist with a monopoly on influence peddling and with whom no one could seriously hope to compete. Some of these stories are apocryphal; others are so exceptional as to demonstrate the truth of the rule that hard work, not personal influence, is the most important factor in a successful lobbying campaign. This is not to suggest that a lifetime of building contacts on the Hill and in the administrative agencies will not be rewarding. Personal relationships built upon years of trust can gain access and credibility for an experienced lobbyist that may not come readily to the neophyte. Any good professional lobbyist will carefully nurture such personal relationships and use them sparingly. It is important to distinguish, however, between access and action. An "old Washington hand" may be able to walk into a number of congressmen's offices and greet the members by their first names. Although impressive and unquestionably useful, few successful lobbying campaigns start or end with this talent. Thus, in deciding whether or not you need a professional, look first to your own ability to spend the time necessary to adequately administer a campaign in Washington. Next, check your finances to determine whether you can afford a professional. Finally, recognize in advance that professional lobbyists are not shamans. They cannot work miracles for you and will borrow your clout to make your case on the Hill. In short, few if any professional lobbyists have a significant degree of personal political power. They can, however, help maximize the power you have through their contacts and credibility, built up over the years.

How Much Will It Cost?

Asking how much a professional lobbyist will cost is like asking how much a car costs: it depends on what you want, a stripped-down compact or a fully loaded Mercedes. Between these extremes, however, there is a wide range where cost and quality are not necessarily related. There are as many Edsels in the lobbying field as in any other area; a six-figure fee does not guarantee Rolls-Royce quality.

The two basic methods of charging lobbying clients are a flat fee or retainer and an hourly rate. Some firms, especially independent lobbying consultants, may insist upon a flat fee; others, particularly lawyers, may agree to an hourly rate.

When you first retain a professional lobbyist, it is almost always to your advantage to request an hourly charge at the outset. A flat-fee arrangement, particularly if it includes expenses, is an open invitation to the lobbyist to cut costs so that she can maximize her profits. Often a flat fee will also encourage a lobbyist to spend as little time as possible on your project. Although some flat-fee proponents argue that this system could just as easily work to the advantage of a client who succeeded in negotiating a low flat fee and then demanded extensive services, this rarely happens. A flat fee arrangement has the advantage of predictability, thus simplifying the drawing up of a lobbying budget. This is difficult to do until you have a sense of what you can expect from a lobbyist and at what price. Thus it is usually best if you start on an hourly basis and graduate to a fixed-fee formula.

How to Choose a Professional Lobbyist

You have decided that neither you nor anyone in your group can afford the time necessary to administer a lobbying campaign in Washington. You have met with your members and have decided to retain a professional to assist you, recognizing that your group will be working with whomever you select on a regular basis and that you're not merely turning over the problem to him. How do you go about finding someone who meets both your needs and your budget? Lobbyists are not listed under their own heading in the Yellow Pages, and even the reference books cited in Chapter 19 will be of little use to you in compiling a list of potential candidates. This is odd considering the thousands of people in Washington who would be anxious to undertake the responsibility of representing your cause.

There are three types of organizations in Washington that regularly accept representation of lobbying matters for special interest groups: law firms, public relations agencies, and specialized lobbying firms. Each of these has its advantages and drawbacks, and you may decide to retain more than one for different needs.

Law Firms

There are more than thirty-five thousand lawyers in Washington; they *are* listed in the Yellow Pages, as well as in such legal directories as *Martindale-Hubbell*. Although the legal directories provide somewhat greater detail than mere listings in the Yellow Pages, even the biographies contained in *Martindale-Hubbell* do not provide a reasonable basis for selecting a law firm and can be deceptive on important issues.

You should recognize that law firms in Washington serve a different function than such firms anywhere else in the country. Many firms in Washington have the attitude that if all else fails, get the law changed. They are less likely to recommend litigation than firms in cities more attuned to the traditional role of lawyers.

Washington lawyers are a special breed of attorney. A significant number have never appeared in court nor opened a law book in years. They know nothing more than the layman about such traditionally legal issues as wills, divorces, taxes, or how to present a case to a jury. Their livelihood is strictly predicated upon their knowledge of the Washington political system that, some would say, has little to do with the law *or* justice. Despite their lack of traditional legal skills, these lawyers can sometimes provide the best representation to private interest groups. In the first place, most lawyer-lobbyists are members of law firms that provide a wide range of legal and extralegal services to their clients. Thus lawyer-lobbyists are able to avail themselves of expertise within their own organization on legal questions with which they are not familiar. For example, a lawyer-lobbyist may be working on changes in a particular piece of legislation and can call upon other more traditionally oriented attorneys in her firm to provide legal analyses of the way existing law has been interpreted by the courts. In many circumstances, this is an invaluable advantage. Many lawyer-lobbyists also can claim a legal specialization in which they are competent to analyze the technical legal aspects of a given problem. The point remains, however, that lawyer-lobbyists are rarely general practitioners and are not what you would ordinarily expect of legal counsel.

By far, most interest groups with outside lobbying assistance are represented by law firms. This being the case, a good starting point for selecting a law firm to represent your interests is to contact trade associations, unions, or other groups with interests and objectives similar to your own and ask them whether they are represented by Washington counsel and how satisfied they are with the service vis-à-vis the costs they have incurred. It is a good idea to contact six or seven of these groups and compile a list of every firm mentioned. Do not drop a firm merely because you receive one bad report. Trade associations are intensely political. Often personal considerations play a part in bad ratings of a particular firm. It should also be emphasized that, although you will generally retain a law firm to represent you, you will almost certainly not have contact with everyone there. One or more individuals within a firm will be given responsibility for your matters. While a firm may have a good (or bad) reputation for representing clients, you should withhold judgment until you actually have an opportunity to meet the individuals who would handle your matters.

Once you have compiled your list of law firms, you should arrange with the senior members of your group, or a committee selected for this purpose, to go to Washington. Do not contact any law firm until you have arranged a convenient time for your own people to travel to the capital. If you have regular meetings, you may wish to have the candidates travel to you. This alternative is less desirable because the lawyers may charge you a fee to attend an out-of-town meeting. Be sure you clarify this before you invite them.

Once you have arranged a convenient time for your people to be in Washington, call the firms on your list. In your inquiries with the trade associations, you should have secured for each firm the name of at least one attorney with whom they regularly dealt. Try him first. If he is not there, ask to speak with one of his associates (in a law firm, *associate* means junior attorney). Explain who you are to the attorney with whom you speak and that you would like to meet with him on a specific day. Most firms will be pleased to arrange their schedules around yours. If you have given adequate notice (at least ten days) and the firm seems reluctant to have anyone meet with you at the time you request, immediately strike it from your list. Remember, you are the client, and it is the firm's obligation to adjust its schedule accordingly. It would be unreasonable to expect, of course, that the individual attorney with whom you originally spoke will, in every case, be able to meet with you at your convenience. If he is any good at all he will probably have other clients who demand similar attention.

It is important to select a firm that is professional enough to provide someone in authority to meet with you at your convenience and who is adequately briefed on your matters. This usually means you will seek out firms with at least two or three attorneys. You need not, however, go to extremes. A firm of six or seven attorneys is often as fully capable of delivering top-quality service as one with hundreds. Size becomes important only to the extent that there is always someone available to you—quite literally on a twenty-four-hour basis. If a firm is unwilling or unable even to discuss matters with a potential new client, its lawyers may already be so overworked that they are not interested in you as a client. You have a right to expect both courtesy and restrained enthusiasm from the outset.

You should count on an interview schedule of two to four firms per day. Start your schedule in the morning with a meeting of your own people at breakfast. All of them should be carefully briefed on what you're looking for and the schedule of events. The interviews should be conducted in the offices of the prospective law firms. This will give you a chance to get a feel for the people with whom you will be working. You should be prepared to give the attorneys a general briefing on the nature of your work, as well as the statistical basis for your claims. One way to judge the enthusiasm of the firm for your cause is by the amount of background research, if any, they have done prior to your meeting. If they are diligent, they will have done at least some cursory research on your issue and should be able to listen intelligently. It would be a mistake, however, to expect them to have as thorough a knowledge of your problem as you have.

After you have described the pertinent issues, ask the attorneys with whom you are meeting how they would approach a lobbying campaign for your cause. Give them an opportunity to fully explain their methodology, then ask as many relevant questions as possible. Do not be reluctant to put them on the spot. Better that you discover now their inadequacies than later, after you have incurred thousands of dollars in billings.

At these interviews, try to be as cynical as courtesy will permit. It would be wise for at least two or three of your own members to be present at such interviews; their impressions may be different than yours. It is also advisable, in picking your selection committee, to choose the most hard-bitten, objective members. Silver-tongued Washington lawyers can impress the gullible all too easily. This advice is the most likely to be ignored in this entire book. We all think we can take care of ourselves, but you're dealing with pros here. Don't trust just your own judgment—rely upon the cumulative impressions of the entire interview committee.

You may be invited to lunch during the interview process. This is a traditional Washington ploy, so do not be overly impressed. You should, however, save your money when the check comes around. If a firm is really anxious to represent your group, the attorneys you are meeting with will usually pick up the tab. If they don't, store that in the back of your mind and graciously accept it yourself.

During the course of the interviews, you should ask the attorneys about other lobbying efforts in which they have been involved and the people with whom they have dealt in groups similar to your own. You should follow up on these remarks after the conclusion of your interview schedule. These groups, some of which may not be familiar to you, may have impressions of the firm different from those which originally referred you to the law firm. You should also ask for an opportunity to meet with those in the firm with whom you would be working. The senior partner you meet with will probably not be involved in your day-to-day matters. The people you will be working with more closely must also be competent and should have a personal rapport with your members. As was the case with legislative assistants, these are the people with whom you will have the most contact.

Finally, and this applies to all the types of lobbyists you might consider retaining, you should discuss money. Do not be surprised if the lawyers with whom you speak are reluctant to be precise about the costs of a lobbying campaign. After all, they are not yet totally familiar with either your organization or the difficulties they may encounter as the campaign progresses. You should, however, be able to get a general estimate of total costs. It is best if you do not indicate to the firm whether you think their rough estimate is high, low, or just about right. This is not the time for bickering; that will come later.

At the conclusion of the interview, whether you think it went well or poorly, you should request a written proposal from the firm regarding their ability to perform the work necessary, their strategy, and their estimate of total costs. It is unlikely that you will receive a proposal for a "contingent fee" from a law firm on lobbying matters. There are serious ethical questions posed when a lawyer accepts contingent fees for the passage or defeat of particular legislation. If a firm *does* offer a contingent-fee relationship, do not suggest to them that it is unethical for them to do so, but merely express your surprise that a firm would make such an offer when it was your understanding that there were significant ethical questions that might arise. This should give you an opportunity to see how fast you can get your prospective representatives to blush.

Law firms offer the greatest variety of representation and in most cases can provide you with the service you need at a reasonable cost. After comparing all the firms both on the basis of your personal interviews and their written proposals, you should present your group with two or three alternatives and conduct a final round of interviews. By this time, the firms should have been thoroughly briefed and you will be in a better position to make an objective choice. Once you have made your decision, however, do not be reluctant to insist that your attorneys continue to represent you aggressively. Remember, they are working for you, not the other way around.

Public Relations Firms

Some public relations firms in Washington offer lobbying services. Although they cannot provide the legal services often so indispensable to a lobbying campaign, they can sometimes give your group the visibility a traditional Washington law firm cannot. Public relations firms generally can generate press coverage, either in the form of paid advertisements or press conferences—something few law firms are qualified to do. If you believe the best way to reach the target audience is through the media, you should at least consider retention of a public relations firm either individually or as an adjunct to other lobbying efforts.

Many public relations firms promote themselves as traditional lobbyists, as well as media specialists; but such firms are the exception. Currently, there are no more than a few dozen individuals at public relations firms who can hope to compete with the better lawyer-lobbyists on the Hill. Although the lawyer-lobbyists can offer legal services in addition to their lobbying skills, the public relations person may possess a more valuable skill: the ability to reach the press.

As with law firms, you should inquire among groups similar to your own about their public relations contacts and conduct interviews similar to those that you would for selecting a law firm. Generally, the presentations given by public relations firms will be much slicker than those of the law firms and may include graphics and dazzling displays of media wizardry. If you are impressed, just be sure to ask what the cost will be for *your* media campaign.

Independent Lobbying Firms

No one has compiled an accurate listing of all the independent lobbying firms in Washington and, as noted earlier, you will not find them listed in the Yellow Pages. They often prefer to be known as "legislative consultants," "management relations firms," or some other euphemism. The best way to find these firms is to be referred by companies or trade associations that have used them in the past. Usually major corporations and trade associations are more than willing to give you the name of the independent lobbyists with whom they have worked.

Independent lobbyists are usually not attorneys, but have Hill or business experience few lawyers can match. It is not unusual to find independent lobbying firms staffed by ex-congressmen and trade association executives with generations of practical legislative experience behind them. Although some lawyers would have you believe the legislative process is so complicated that only a law degree properly qualifies an individual to analyze pending or proposed legislation, the success of independent lobbying firms is proof to the contrary.

Independent lobbying firms often offer the additional advantage of a package deal where all legislative matters of an individual client will be undertaken for a flat fee. Most lawyers operate on an hourly or retainer basis with expenses added. You may be better able to accurately predict costs with an independent lobbying firm.

As with law firms and public relations agencies, independent lobbying firms are often known for having a particular political orientation. Some are more effective in Democratic administrations and others during Republican years. Be sure to request résumés of all firm members who would be working on your matters before you make any decisions. Just because an independent firm may have a particular political strength (or weakness), you should *never* make your decision about retaining them solely on that basis. Washington is a transient town, and no effective lobbying organization will be around long if it has not demonstrated its ability to change with the times. Thus, a Republican may be able to effectively represent your issue even if you believe it would be a more Democratic issue. Remember, party labels are highly deceptive; conservative Democrats often vote with Republicans and liberal Republicans with Democrats.

Independent firms may offer political experience that is as valuable as the legal expertise you can expect from a law firm or the publicity know-how you receive from a public relations firm. It is here that the importance of the personal contact comes in. Unlike most lawyers, members of independent lobbying firms often have access to the Senate or House floor if they are ex-members. This gives them an advantage in last-minute lobbying.

Some lobbying groups cover themselves by retaining independent lobbying firms, law firms, *and* public relations agencies. Although this may be a safe way of covering all the bases, it can be incredibly expensive. If you decide to go this route, you should be sure all the groups you have working for you get along with one another on a personal as well as a professional basis. You don't need to waste your time or money paying for the working out of the professional jealousies of various competing firms. It is therefore important that you specify *in writing*, to all the parties, the functions of all groups working for you. If you choose to go this route, it is also an excellent idea to spend as much time as possible coordinating or at least overseeing the coordination of their activities. Bills can mount rapidly when you have a number of meters running, and some who feel hurt about not being engaged exclusively would have no compunction about sending their client an inflated bill.

In short, independent lobbying agencies can offer some services generally unavailable from either law firms or public relations firms. They are a good idea if you want the inside political track and a fixed fee. If they believe the risk is good, you may be able to get a results-oriented campaign with real motivation driving your consultant.

Aside from the contingent-fee arrangement, you should be highly skeptical of any professional lobbyist who guarantees a particular result. Lobbying and legislation are just too uncertain a game for this to be possible.

Eighteen

★ ★ ★ ★ ★

The Ten Commandments

★ ★ ★ ★

Bad laws are the worst sort of tyranny.

—Edmund Burke

Although the role of a lobbyist may appear extremely complex,* the citizen lobbyist can be effective by following a few simple rules.

1. Know Your Facts and Be Accurate in Expressing Them

Despite the myth that successful lobbying implies influence peddling, most effective lobbyists trade in facts—not influence. What citizen lobbyists may lack in experience and contacts they can compensate for in knowledge and research. Accuracy and thoroughness are the hallmarks of successful lobbying campaigns.

During the course of any emotionally charged campaign, there is always a temptation to overstate your case, manufacture statistics to fit your argument, or misrepresent your opponents' views. Succumbing to these temptations is almost always ruinous. Even if you win the

---

* This book does not even attempt to consider such sophisticated issues as congressional parliamentary procedure, fund-raising, compliance with the Foreign Agents Registration Act of 1938, and myriad other topics.

battle, you may lose the war. Your long-term credibility is far more important than any temporary advantage you may gain through provocation.

2. Know Your Opposition

For every political cause, there will be political opposition. Effective lobbyists will identify their opposition early in a lobbying campaign, fairly and accurately analyze the arguments and power sources of their opposition, and attempt to neutralize them. At least as much time should be devoted to analysis and repudiation of your opponents' position as in developing your own case. Again, the watchword of a consistently successful lobbyist is honesty and accuracy. Mischaracterizations of an opponent's position can be as damaging to your own credibility as misstatements of fact in arguing your own case. Rebuttal of opposing positions should go only so far as is necessary to counter your opponents' lobbying effort. You do not need to make their case for them, but be prepared to give two licks for every one you receive.

3. Correct Errors Immediately

Although all lobbyists attempt to be 100 percent accurate in every document or statement they make, errors inevitably creep in. This can result from the passage of time, changes in the facts themselves, or simple misinterpretations of statistics, dates, legal citations, and so on. And the more individuals participating in a lobbying campaign, the more likely errors will occur. Thus it is essential for your organization to have firm policies regarding the individuals authorized to speak for the group, the types of commitments these individuals are permitted to make on behalf of the group, the literature and statistics upon which your group bases its arguments, and the procedures to be followed when errors occur.

Mistakes should be corrected as soon as possible after they are discovered. It is not enough merely to admit that a mistake was made; your organization must also supply the accurate information at the time it corrects its error. Finally, your degree of public acknowledgment of the error should be dictated by the seriousness of the mistake. Usually, warning the recipients of the inaccurate information that it should not be relied upon and correcting the mistake in as low-key a manner as possible will be enough. It is always embarrassing to admit you're wrong, but it is political suicide if you don't. You can put a good face on errors, but do not attempt to cover them up, particularly if your allies are relying upon the information you have supplied.

4. Plan, Coordinate, and Follow Up on Each Contact

An enormous amount of time, energy, and intellect is wasted each year by lobbyists who have not carefully planned their approach to the Hill. Each contact you make with a congressional office should be thoroughly researched in advance, careful notes should be kept of the content and results of meetings, and each meeting should be followed up with additional *written* memoranda.

It does a lobbyist little good to develop a network of congressional allies and then not use them. Friends should be kept fully informed of your activities, their questions and comments should be promptly addressed and, above all, they must be thanked for their contribution to your cause. Your skill and diligence in using your contacts will be a measure of your success.

5. Avoid Zealotry

The more strongly you feel about an issue, the more important it is to be aware of the danger of zealotry. Fanaticism neither impresses nor convinces many people in Washington. Symptomatic of zealotry are misrepresenting your opponents' views; underestimating your opposition; believing—and saying—that your opponents are motivated by unethical and even immoral instincts; and, finally, overstating your own case. Zealotry is the enemy of credibility, the lobbyist's greatest asset. It is one thing to be an aggressive advocate, quite another to replace rational argument with slogans.

6. Cultivate Your Allies; Make Sure They Do Their Part

There is hardly an issue in Washington that does not attract or repel a number of groups for widely different reasons. Your chances of succeeding in a lobbying campaign will be enormously enhanced if you join with other groups who share your aims. Allies don't just happen; they must be sought out and cultivated. In the nation's capital you are likely to find them in the most unlikely places—even among groups that have traditionally opposed you. In seeking allies, keep your eye on the ultimate objective of the lobbying campaign, not the positions or personalities of your allies. Few political objectives worth achieving can be gained without allies of some sort.

Merely gaining allies, however, is not enough. You must be sure they do their part. Specifically, make sure your friends keep their promises and abide by the same standards of credibility and integrity you set for yourself. Announce in writing specific goals and projects each group will be expected to perform. Make sure you keep your part of the deal and they keep theirs.

7. Know the Legislative Process

All the good intentions, careful planning, research, and alliances will do you little good unless you are familiar with the legislative process. These are the rules by which the game is played. At the least, you should be conversant with the system by which bills become laws and are translated into administrative action. Few people, even members of Congress, are regarded as parliamentary experts on all aspects of congressional procedure, but as a lobbyist you have an obligation to be at least as familiar with the rules as the people employing them on the floor of the Senate and the House. It is equally important that you understand what happens to laws after they are passed. Often, the clear intent of the Congress is subverted by overly (or underly) zealous bureaucrats. You can affect neither legislation nor the way it is administered unless you are thoroughly familiar with the game.

8. Be Frugal with Your Money

You have no doubt read of professional lobbying campaigns costing hundreds of thousands of dollars. These are mounted by sophisticated pressure groups with more money than good sense. Be very judicious about how you spend your funds. This is particularly true when you must retain outside consultants or attorneys. Sometimes they are absolutely necessary, but be sure you get your money's worth.

9. Grow Thick Skin

You don't have to be a cynic to be a successful Washington lobbyist, but a healthy degree of skepticism helps. You also should develop an immunity to petty insults, you must not allow temporary setbacks to ruin your concentration, and you must not take any of the attacks on your position personally. You must understand that the fire aimed in your direction is merely business. Although you should take your job seriously, you can't afford to take *yourself* too seriously in a lobbying campaign. Above all, maintain your sense of humor. You'll need it.

10. Win

No one should become involved in lobbying as an academic exercise. This is serious business that can affect thousands of people's lives and the way our country is run. People in Washington don't necessarily object to amateurs, but you will find few who will tolerate those who abuse the rights of petition and redress. Since you are expected to take your role seriously, one of the hallmarks of this attitude is a dedication to winning and not merely "playing the game." One of the rules of this game is a commitment to your cause. No matter how futile your chances of success may appear, you must not deviate from your commitment. This is one factor that separates the citizen lobbyist from the professional. Some career lobbyists are merely hired guns who go from one issue to the next with little personal stake in the outcome. Citizen lobbyists are almost always deeply committed individuals who really *believe* in what they are doing. Strength of conviction is what offsets the enormous financial advantage enjoyed by some of the huge special interest lobbies. Not only that, but winning is always more fun than losing.

Nineteen

★ ★ ★ ★ ★

Resources

★ ★ ★ ★ ★

The purpose of this book was to give you a general idea of lobbying techniques. It is only an instruction manual; to do an adequate job at lobbying you will need the proper tools. This chapter is designed to help you choose the right tools for the job.

Seminars

The *Congressional Quarterly* conducts seminars entitled "Congress and the Legislative Process." These half-day and one-day workshops stress the basic workings of Congress and are extremely valuable both for the novice and intermediate lobbyist. For further information contact:

Seminar Coordinator
Congressional Quarterly, Inc.
1414 22nd Street, N.W.
Washington, D.C. 20037
Cost: $295 (half day only)

"How Our Laws Are Made" is a pamphlet printed by the government and distributed through most congressional offices. Although the text is written at an eighth-grade level, this book is a remarkably comprehensive analysis of the legislative process. It should be required reading for anyone not thoroughly familiar with the procedures of the Congress. To get a copy, merely write to your congressman or senator and request it. There should be no charge.

Reference Manuals

Congressional Directory

This book is published by the Government Printing Office and provides a biography of all members of Congress, a list of their committee assignments and committee staffs, a cross-index of staffs, and congressional district maps. Almost every lobbyist's office in Washington has these directories, but better manuals are published through private sources. About the only thing unique about the *Congressional Directory* is the section with congressional district maps. Congressional staffs change so rapidly that, by the time the *Congressional Directory* is published, it is out of date. At the price, however, it is a good starting point; it is a traditional part of every lobbyist's library. Copies of the *Congressional Directory* may be ordered from:

Government Printing Office
710 N. Capitol Street, N.W.
Washington, D.C. 20401
(202) 653–5075
Cost: $23.00

Congressional Staff Directory

The *Congressional Staff Directory* is privately published and provides a more thorough cross-indexing of congressional offices, committee assignments, and so on than does the *Congressional Directory*. Although it lacks the congressional district maps, it is generally a more useful reference manual than the *Congressional Directory* insofar as congressmen themselves are concerned. The *Congressional Staff Directory* may be ordered from:

Congressional Staff Directory
P.O. Box 62
Mt. Vernon, VA 22121
(703) 739–0900
Cost: $79.00

Almanac of American Politics

The *Almanac of American Politics* provides a reasonably comprehensive analysis of each member of Congress, including a thumbnail sketch of the congressman's district, voting record, and ratings by various interest groups. These groups' ratings (such as Americans for Constitutional Action [ACA], Americans for Democratic Action [ADA]) will give you an idea of the congressman's basic proclivity—moderate, liberal, conservative. Do not, however, be dissuaded from approaching a congressman merely because his general voting pattern may not seem friendly to your cause. The *Almanac* should merely serve as a guide to the political leanings of congressmen. The *Almanac of American Politics* is unique in the type of analysis it provides and is an extremely valuable resource tool. It may be ordered from Random House. Its list price is $49.95.

Congressional Yellow Book

The *Congressional Yellow Book* is a loose-leaf binder published by Leadership Directories, Inc. Its format provides for easy updating of changes on congressional staff and committee assignments. Since these occur with what some would regard as alarming regularity, the *Congressional Yellow Book* is probably the most useful day-to-day resource book you can have in your library. Although it is relatively expensive, it can save you hours in tracking down the right staff member for your problem. The *Congressional Yellow Book* also includes information on all special interest caucuses (such as the Black Caucus and the Steel Caucus), unavailable in a similar format in any other publication. In short, the *Congressional Yellow Book* is the single most valuable tool you can have and is highly recommended. It can be ordered from:

Leadership Directories, Inc.
1301 Pennsylvania Avenue, N.W.; Suite 925
Washington, D.C. 20004
(202) 347–7757
Cost: $250.00/year

Federal Yellow Book

The *Federal Yellow Book* is also published by Leadership Directories, Inc. It provides up-to-date listings of virtually the entire federal bureaucracy. Its loose-leaf format enables you to update it on a regular basis, and it is very useful in attempting to penetrate the maze of the bureaucracy. Although it is somewhat intimidating in appearance, it is much easier to use than the official government telephone books and is accurate about 80 percent of the time—a remarkable achievement given the constant changes within the bureaucracy. If any significant portion of your lobbying activities involves contacts within the administrative branch, the *Federal Yellow Book* is a must. To order contact:

Leadership Directories, Inc.
1301 Pennsylvania Avenue, N.W.; Suite 925
Washington, D.C. 20004
(202) 347–7757
Cost: $250.00/year

Standing Rules of the United States Senate; Standing Rules of the United States House of Representatives

These two publications are the equivalent of *Robert's Rules of Order* for the House and the Senate. Each body has its own rules, which differ in significant respects. Do not attempt to read these books cover to cover. A literal reading is almost inherently misleading. They're useful when part of your tactics involve sophisticated parliamentary maneuvering and belong on your resource shelf to be consulted when necessary. One caveat: The rules of the House and Senate are subject to change, so you should be sure to get the current year's version. These manuals are available from:

Clerk
United States House of Representatives
Washington, D.C. 20515
Cost: free

Secretary
United States Senate
Washington, D.C. 20510
Cost: free

Congressional Districts By Zip

In preparing any grassroots letter-writing campaign, it is essential that you know which congressmen represent your constituents. In cases where there is only one congressman (such as North Dakota), the job is relatively easy. In more populous areas, however, it is extremely difficult to determine exactly where your constituents have their greatest concentration vis-à-vis congressional districts. *CD* (Congressional Districts) *By Zip* provides a CD-ROM cross-reference for this problem and lists all the zip codes in a given congressional district. All you have to do to determine where your greatest power lies is match your constituents' zip codes to those listed in the database. *CD By Zip* is absolutely essential if you plan to do any grassroots lobbying or undertake letter-writing campaigns. It is available from:

Congressional Quarterly Staff Directories, Inc.
P.O. Box 62
Mt. Vernon, VA 22121
(703) 739–0900
Cost: $2,500 for a five-digit one year data-use license with
a six-month update
$1,500 for a five-digit one year data-use license

Government Affairs Yellow Book

This soft-bound directory lists most of the major special interest groups in Washington, together with their addresses, telephone numbers, and principal representatives. The *Government Affairs Yellow Book* is cross-indexed by representatives and clients so that you can determine, for example, which law firms represent whom. Although the *Government Affairs Yellow Book* is about the most thorough available, it is *not* comprehensive. In fact, it barely scratches the surface of the labyrinthine world of Washington representation. Further, the *Government Affairs Yellow Book* is replete with errors, so it cannot be relied upon as definitive. Still, it's the best such directory available, and you should have one in your library. To order a copy, contact:

Leadership Directories, Inc.
1301 Pennsylvania Avenue, N.W.; Suite 925
Washington, D.C. 20004
Cost: $190/year
(202) 347–7757

News Media Yellow Book

The *News Media Yellow Book* lists all media correspondents by the publication they represent, and it is cross-indexed. This is an indispensable tool if you are planning any sort of media campaign, and it should provide you with a good starting point for developing a list for press releases. It is available from:

Leadership Directories, Inc.
1301 Pennsylvania Avenue, N.W.; Suite 925
Washington, D.C. 20004
(202)347-7757
Cost: $250/year

Pocket Manuals

Pocket manuals of congressional organization are available from a number of trade associations and labor unions. Any attempt to enumerate all of them would invariably miss some, so prospective lobbyists should first inquire with their own trade associations or interest groups to see whether a specialized pocket manual has been produced by them. Some of the better-known manuals are published by the United States Chamber of Commerce, the AFL–CIO, and the American Mining Congress. These books are sometimes available only to association or union members, but a direct inquiry is often rewarded. These pocket manuals are much handier than the reference books cited previously and can be carried in your pocket or purse. Inquiries about the manuals may be addressed to:

Chamber of Commerce of the U.S.A.
1615 H Street, N.W.
Washington, D.C. 20062

AFL–CIO
815 16th Street, N.W.
Washington, D.C. 20006

National Mining Association
1130 17th St., N.W.
Washington, D.C. 20036

Government Periodicals and Subscription Services

The *Government Periodicals and Subscription Services* is published by the Government Printing Office (GPO). It contains a complete listing of all current publications of the GPO, cross-indexed by title and subject matter. In presenting any lobbying campaign on the Hill, government studies and data are usually given great credibility. Predictably, you should be able to find a government publication supporting virtually any position you wish to take. The catalog is published regularly, so it would be a good idea to be placed on the regular mailing list for new publications. Government publications are reasonably priced and can be procured either in person or by mail. For further information contact:

Government Printing Office
710 N. Capitol Street, N.W.
Washington, D.C. 20401
(202) 653–5075

Periodicals

Congressional Quarterly Weekly Report

The *Congressional Quarterly Weekly Report* is probably one of the periodicals relied upon most by Washington insiders. Although it is relatively expensive, its articles on the status of legislation, on personalities, and on committee jurisdiction—as well as the other information essential to an effective lobbying campaign that it provides—are not duplicated by any other publication. It is well worth the cost. For subscription information contact:

Congressional Quarterly Weekly Report
1414 22nd Street, N.W.
Washington, D.C. 20037
(202) 887–8515
Cost: $1,435/year

Bureau of National Affairs

The Bureau of National Affairs (BNA) is a nonpartisan research organization that publishes a number of specialized newsletters (such as *Environmental Law Reporter, Import Weekly*) in almost all fields affected directly by legislation. The BNA reports, although rather costly, include specialized information on topics of interest to your group that you will be unable to find in most other publications. To receive a full list of current BNA publications along with descriptions, sample issues, and a price list, write to:

The Bureau of National Affairs, Inc.
1231 25th Street, N.W.
Washington, D.C. 20037
(202) 452–4200

CQ Monitor

The *CQ Monitor* (formerly the *Congressional Monitor*) is a daily update of pending congressional action. This publication is useful if you
are tracking four or five pieces of legislation; it gives you advance
notice of all pending hearings, mark-up sessions, and votes. Its format is clearer than any government publication. Although the *CQ
Monitor* attempts to be comprehensive, the vagaries of committee
chairmen mean that this publication is not infallible. Still, if you need
to track legislation on a current basis, the *CQ Monitor* is excellent.
For further information contact:

CQ Monitor
1414 22nd St., N.W.
Washington, D.C. 20037
(202) 887–8515
Cost: $1,495/year

National Journal

The *National Journal* is a specialized political publication with its
greatest readership in the Washington area, particularly among lobbyists. Like the *Congressional Quarterly Weekly Report*, the *National
Journal* concentrates on in-depth stories regarding pending and proposed legislation, status of committee and subcommittee action, hard
news about political personalities, and other stories useful to lobbyists. In addition, *National Journal* provides a summary of committee
action and legislative calendars. These are sometimes more up-to-
date than even the back pages of the *Congressional Record*, which
purports to carry the same information. The *National Journal* also
includes analyses of administrative action and is well worth its relatively high price. For further information contact:

National Journal
1730 M Street, N.W.
Washington, D.C.
(202) 739–8400
Cost: $439.00/year

Study Committees and Special Interest Caucuses

On both sides of the Congress, several study and/or policy committees, as well as special interest caucuses, publish analyses of pending and proposed legislation. These analyses are usually slanted toward the view of the particular committee or caucus concerned; but that is sometimes what you want. Many of the privately published journals are neutral in tone. This is fine when you are preparing your facts, but you also have to know the arguments on both sides of the question. To find out what your supporters and opponents are saying on the Hill, contact the relevant special interest caucus or study group. Although a few are listed below, check the *Congressional Yellow Book* to see if a special interest caucus has been recently formed in your field. The following are the best-known groups:

Senate Republican Policy Committee
333 Russell Senate Office Building
Washington, D.C. 20510
(202) 224–2946

Senate Democratic Policy Committee
S–118 Capitol Building
Washington, D.C. 20510
(202) 224–5551

House Democratic Steering and Policy Committee
114 House Office Building Annex 1
Washington, D.C. 20515
(202) 225–0100

House Republican Policy Committee
1620 Longworth House Office Building
Washington, D.C. 20515
(202) 225–6168

Democratic Study Group
1422 Longworth House Office Building
Washington, D.C. 20515
(202) 225–5858

Whip Notices

The majority and minority parties of both houses publish so-called whip notices on a daily basis during the legislative session. These are relied upon extensively by professional lobbyists because they indicate what the congressional leadership (i.e. whips) thinks will happen during a particular legislative day. (A whip is a political manager, elected by his party colleagues, whose job it is to assure attendance of his party members at votes and more. The name implies that, as a party officer, this person "whips" his members into line.)

Although whip notices are available by mail, their real value lies in immediacy. You would be well advised to have whip notices picked up by your messenger if you are in the thick of a legislative duel. They're available from:

Senate Majority Whip
S–148 Capitol Building
Washington, D.C. 20510
(202) 224–2708

Senate Minority Whip
S–229 Capitol Building
Washington, D.C. 20510
(202) 224–2158

House Majority Whip
H–107 Capitol Building
Washington, D.C. 20515
(202) 225–0197

House Minority Whip
2112 Rayburn House Office Building
Washington, D.C. 20515
(202) 225–3130

Trade Association and Interest Group Publications

In Washington virtually every trade association and special interest group with a membership of more than three has a trade publication. Sometimes these publications are limited to members, but often membership costs are low enough to justify joining just to receive the

publication. Publications range from the sophisticated to the juvenile. You would be well advised to review a copy or two before you
make the decision to subscribe. At some point, some interest groups
start publishing their own weekly or monthly newsletter using the
sources described in this chapter, as well as their own information.
For further information, contact the trade associations listed in the
trade association directories noted earlier in this chapter.

Magazines, Newspapers, and Newsletters

Special Interest Publications

At last count, there were over fifteen thousand newspapers, magazines, and newsletters being published in the United States on subjects
ranging from sky diving to embryology. No matter how arcane your
subject, most likely there is at least one publication that specializes in
it. Even if you disagree with the editorial policies of the publication in
your field, it is always a good idea to subscribe. After all, you should
know even the myths that are being circulated about your subject.
Often, free copies of these publications are distributed on the Hill.

Newspapers of Note

In addition to the specialized publications, most Washington lobbyists begin their morning by reading the *Washington Post, The New York
Times,* and *The Wall Street Journal.* Even if you believe that your issue
is not likely to be covered in depth by these publications, they contain
politically sensitive stories that few effective lobbyists can afford to
ignore. For subscription information contact:

Washington Post
1150 15th Street, N.W.
Washington, D.C. 20071

The New York Times
1000 Connecticut Avenue, N.W.
Washington, D.C. 20036

The Wall Street Journal
11501 Columbia Pike
Silver Springs, MD 20904

Kiplinger Washington Newsletter

The Kiplinger letter is one of the most highly advertised newsletters in Washington. Its sparse style and immediacy set it apart from other similar publications. Kiplinger also publishes a number of specialized newsletters that follow the same style and content. Although not specifically designed for lobbyists, the Kiplinger letter provides fast, usually accurate thumbnail advisories on issues that may be important to you. For further information contact:

Kiplinger Washington Newsletter
1729 H Street, N.W.
Washington, D.C. 20006

Governmental Material

During the course of any lobbying campaign, you will need a small library on the current law, applicable regulations, and the legislative history of existing statutes. These are all available from government sources at prices significantly below those offered by private companies. Although there are numerous services that will provide you with in-depth, sophisticated resource documents, you will usually be best advised to get this information from the government itself. The documents described below are needed in any lobbying campaign.

Congressional Record

The *Congressional Record* is literally the minutes of congressional debates. It is published daily during the congressional sessions, and for its bulk (three to four hundred pages a day), it is relatively inexpensive. You should take out a subscription to the *Congressional Record* rather than try to pick it up on an ad hoc basis. Mail takes two days at the minimum, but in the Washington area you can arrange to have the *Congressional Record* delivered to you the "morning after." Few successful lobbying offices in Washington do not get this publication. For a subscription contact:

The Government Printing Office
710 N. Capitol Street, N.W.
Washington, D.C. 20401
Cost: $1.50 per day

Federal Register

The *Federal Register* is published daily, except weekends and holidays, and includes notices from all federal regulatory and administrative agencies. These include notices of administrative hearings, decisions, proposed rules, and all other bureaucratic action. Many of the notices published in the *Federal Register* are required by law and can be legally binding. Even if you feel you are only interested in legislation (as opposed to regulation), you cannot afford to be without the *Federal Register*. Order from:

The Government Printing Office
710 N. Capitol Street, N.W.
Washington, D.C. 20401
Cost: $8.00 per day

United States Code

The *United States Code* (and a privately published version, *United States Code Annotated*) includes the corpus of federal law. The entire set comprises dozens of volumes, but unless you are planning to practice law or are very rich, you need only purchase the volumes that directly affect your area. Because federal law changes so quickly, it is essential that you update your copy on a regular basis. The *United States Code Annotated (USCA)* includes a yearly "pocket" part that slides into the rear cover. *USCA* also provides a cursory legislative history of each title and section of the code and a list of court cases explaining each provision of law. *USCA* is a useful tool in determining what the law actually means (despite what it may say), but you should be careful not to rely exclusively upon its opinions. If you have questions regarding the interpretation of legislation, consult an attorney. The *United States Code Annotated* is available from:

West Publishing Company
901 15th St., N.W.
Washington, D.C. 20005
(800) 328 9352

Code of Federal Regulations

The *Code of Federal Regulations* (CFR) incorporates all the technical interpretations of statutes as construed by the bureaucracy and is critical to virtually every lobbying effort. As with the *United States*

Code, you need not purchase all of the *CFR*, but only those volumes that pertain to your particular issue. Most *CFR* titles are republished on an annual basis and reflect changes during the preceding year. *Never* rely upon outdated *CFR*s in presenting your case, because regulations change even more frequently than statutes. Individual volumes of *CFR* may be obtained from:

Government Printing Office
710 N. Capitol Street, N.W.
Washington, D.C. 20401
(202) 512–1800
Cost: $883/year (full set)
Individual copies: $5.00–$9.00

Other Legal Publications

There are literally dozens of publicly and privately published legal treatises, encyclopedias, services, and so on that interpret the existing statutes. Most of these are designed for use by lawyers and are expensive. If you have specific questions on the interpretation of the law, it is usually cheaper and safer to request an attorney to prepare a memorandum of law for you on a specific subject than to attempt to subscribe to all of the services. After all, the lawyer's fee will include the cost of subscribing to these publications, and it is usually cheaper, easier, and faster to get specialized advice at that point.

Undoubtedly, this advice will be challenged not only by publishers of law books, but also by lobbyists who have their own favorite reporting system. As you gain more expertise in the field, undoubtedly you will form your own prejudices.

Clipping Services

In addition to your ordinary subscriptions, a clipping service is sometimes a valuable asset. It will review any publications you select and clip articles pertaining to subjects in which you are interested. These will be sent to you on a daily or weekly basis, as you prefer. The advantage of a clipping service is that it saves you the time entailed in going through numerous publications to which you would not ordinarily subscribe and can save you considerable expense. This is not to say that clipping services are cheap; most services charge a base rate and a separate fee for each article they send you. Clipping services are listed in the Yellow Pages, but you should seek recommendations from people who have used them before you sign any contracts.

Press Services

The Press Relations Wire Service will put your press releases on a nationwide telex system for a fee. Many papers across the country, particularly those in the hustings, will carry these stories as fillers. You can also target the Press Relations Wire Service to focus on specific regions of the country at considerably reduced cost. Contact:

Press Relations Wire
National Press Building
Washington, D.C.
(202) 347–5155

The Law

Hearings and Reports

During the legislative process, the various congressional committees that consider a particular bill will publish transcripts of hearings and other information submitted for the record. These transcripts are available from the Superintendent of Documents or, more easily, from the committee that conducted the hearing. If you order them through the Government Printing Office, there will be a charge (usually less than two dollars), but you can almost always get them free from the committee itself. Unlike the *Congressional Record* and the *Federal Register*, transcripts are published irregularly—usually months after the hearings actually take place. Transcripts of prior hearings are available either from the committee that conducted the hearings, the superintendent of documents, or the Government Printing Office. If you need hearings going back a number of years, you can acquire them from the Library of Congress, but you will have to pay a substantial reproduction fee.

Committee reports are also published irregularly, but usually soon after the responsible committee has made its decisions regarding a piece of legislation. These reports are a much better guide to legislative history than are the transcripts of the hearings because they represent the *intent* of the Congress relating to the legislation in question. Committee reports on legislation affecting your subject matter are an essential part of your library. They can be acquired (usually at no cost) from the committee or the superintendent of documents. A list of available reports is contained in the Congressional Monitor series and in the back of the *Congressional Record.*

Bills and Committee Prints

When a bill is introduced, copies are made available almost immediately to the public at no charge. These are available from the clerk of the House of Representatives and the secretary of the Senate, both located in the Capitol Building. After a bill has been partially "marked up" (see Chapter 8), a revised version of the bill will be published under the designation "committee print." This is available from the document rooms of the House and Senate. The committee print will indicate the original version of the bill by putting a single line through any deleted text and italicizing added text. In tracking the progress of any legislation, it is essential for you to get the most recent version of the proposed legislation. There are delivery services in Washington that will pick them up if you do not have your own messengers. The clerk of the House and secretary of the Senate will also mail you these versions upon request.

Bill Status Offices

Both the House and the Senate maintain offices that analyze the status of all pending bills. The service is free, and you can determine the status of any legislation by calling the Capitol and requesting the respective bill status office. The Capitol telephone number is: (202) 224–3121.

The majority and minority parties in the House and Senate also maintain recorded updates of the status of floor action during the legislative session. These recorded messages are updated several times daily, and you can call on a twenty-four-hour basis. This service is particularly useful in planning last-minute strategy. It is also helpful for getting current information on passage or defeat of legislation. Telephone numbers to call are:

House Republican Cloak Room: (202) 225–7350

House Democratic Cloak Room: (202) 225–7330

Senate Republican Cloak Room: (202) 224–6191

Senate Democratic Cloak Room: (202) 224–4691

Note: many administrative agencies also maintain dial-a-regulation tapes where recent agency action is communicated. Since the telephone numbers for dial-a-regulation tapes change frequently, you should call the main switchboard number of the agency concerned for the current listing.

Services

Delivery Services

Washington is unique in a number of respects, but perhaps the strangest is its reliance upon delivery services. Everything, it seems, must be delivered yesterday. Virtually every law firm with more than five people has its own messenger, and there are at least a dozen private delivery firms that offer two-hour delivery of any package in town. It's not that the mail service is so bad, just that having materials hand-delivered has become a Washington tradition. Messengers are also useful in picking up packages from the Hill, the Superintendent of Documents, the clerk of the House, and secretary of the Senate. Senate and House committees are notorious for not sending promised bills, reports, and so on, and messengers become indispensable. The reliance on messengers is so deeply ingrained in Washington that workers in Hill offices sometimes feel you don't deserve it if you don't pick it up. Some of the better-known messenger services are:

Central Delivery
(301) 953–2777

Republic Express Courier Service
(202) 393–5514

Bankers Couriers, Inc.
(301) 565–0600

Grace Courier Service
(703) 550–5000

Best Messenger Inc.
(202) 986–0100

Trans-Express
(202) 408–8877

Hotels

Washington hotels are overbooked much of the time. Therefore, it is *always* advisable to reserve a room well in advance. Although the ratings of hotels go up and down, prices only go up. Rather than attempt to list all the hotels in Washington, I suggest you write to:

Visitors Information Association
1212 New York Ave., N.W.
Washington, D.C.
(202) 789–7000

They have a comprehensive up-to-date list of all the hotels in the area.

Restaurants

For years, Washington was regarded by epicureans as a gastronomical wasteland. Whether that was ever true is a subject of some debate, but that is certainly not an accurate analysis today. In fact, lunch is a Washington lobbying tradition; you would be well advised to spend as many noon hours as possible in restaurants (always with a congressman, member of the congressional staff, or another lobbyist). A number of excellent restaurant guides are published, perhaps the best being the January issue of *The Washingtonian* magazine that rates the top 100 restaurants. For information call (202) 296–3600.

Metro

The Washington public transportation system includes a subway and buses that are interconnected. Metro, as it is called locally, is by far the fastest and cheapest way to get around town, particularly in winter and during rush hour. If you are familiar with the Chicago L or the New York subway, don't be dismayed. The Washington system is not covered with graffiti; it's clean, fast, and safe. For further information about Metro contact:

Washington Metropolitan Transit
600 5th St., N.W.
Washington, D.C. 20011
(202) 637–7000

Taxis

The Washington cab system is a throwback to another era. Washington taxis operate on the zone system and do not have meters. Each cab carries a zone map behind the driver, but you have to have been born in Washington to decipher it. Fares are relatively inexpensive, but there is ample opportunity for fudging. If you are unfamiliar with the geography, ask the driver *before* you leave how much the fare will be. Under District practice, drivers may pick up other fares on the way to your destination as long as it does not take you more than four blocks out of your way. Your fare will not be affected by picking up other riders, but you may be delayed. Drivers are also reluctant to go to certain destinations in Washington, particularly in the Northeast quadrant and Anacostia. If you must go to one of these areas, get in the cab and close the door—*then* tell the driver where you are going. If he refuses, suggest that you will write to the appropriate authorities. Drivers tend to be more accommodating to forceful people. You should also be aware that during rush hours and "snow emergencies" there is a surcharge. Notwithstanding the complexity of the Washington cab system, taxis are readily available and, because parking on the Hill is impossible, they and Metro have a monopoly on transportation there. If there is any dispute about your fare, do not be reluctant to call the cops. They are very experienced in taxi shakedowns.

Office Space

Washington is one of the tightest real estate markets in the country, with less than 5 percent available office space at any given time. Office space is outrageously expensive in the downtown area (sixteen to forty-five dollars per square foot per year). If you intend setting up an office in Washington, you might initially decide to rent space on Capitol Hill, where rents are somewhat more reasonable and very convenient to both Houses of the Congress. If you plan on a permanent office in Washington, you should consult commercial real estate brokers.

There are also consultants who can help you set up an entire office, including telephones, furniture, stationery, and the thousands of other details that can frustrate even the most temperate people. There are several office planning consultants in Washington whom you can find in the phone book. Be sure to ask before retaining them whether they are "full service," that is, will not only arrange for furniture but will take care of all the other details as well. You should *not* expect an interior designer or office furniture company to perform services outlined here. These office consultants are often recommended through word of mouth, so you should also ask other trade associations about their experiences.

Other Services and Materials

There are several adequate publications listing office materials suppliers and services. These are basically advertising directories, so read the claims with a note of caution. These directories can be secured from:

Greater Washington Board of Trade
1129 20th St., N.W.
Washington, D.C. 20036

Tips for the Computer Literate

Yes, even the government has entered the electronic age. Of course, the Internet was originally a government creation, but many agencies in Washington have been a bit slow in taking advantage of this technology.

Fortunately, that time has passed, and there are now literally hundreds of web sites that provide information. The House and the Senate both have their own home pages, which provide huge amounts of information on members, committees, the legislative process, and so on. The Senate home page is (surprise) http://www.senate.gov and the House can be reached at http://www.house.gov.

Through these home pages, you can download full texts of laws, bills, schedules, and related resources. This is obviously *much* cheaper than subscribing to services, and for the adept, can even be faster.

Voting records of members of Congress are available through THOMAS which is a website operated by the Library of Congress (http://THOMAS.loc.gov/). THOMAS is a good starting point for any research concerning the operation of the federal government. You can link with all sorts of data. To access voting records directly, go to http://lcweb.loc.gov/global/legislative/voting.html.

Another well-known web site that provides access to government information is CapWeb, which can be reached at http://policy.net/capweb/congress.html. Finally there are literally hundreds of government gophers through which you can reach almost any agency in the entire government. Try, gopher://peg.cwis.uci.edu...S%20and%20

government, or gopher://marvel.loc.gov:70/11/congress/gophers, or gopher://peg.cwis.uci.edu...come/peg/GOPHERS/government.

For a full list of government agencies on the Internet, use http://www.lib.lsu.edu/gov/fedgov/html.

Another valuable resource is the Government Printing Office, which has put hundreds of documents including the *Federal Register* on line. This can result in enormous savings over actually purchasing documents. Use http://www.access.gpo.gov/.

Be aware that there is no single government standard as to how pages are put together, or even the format of files. You may need additional software to view some of the files (such as Adobe Acrobat), but that is often available for downloads.

Although the government already offers massive amounts of information on the Internet, its lapses can be frustrating. Since its inception, for example, the House home page has been much more comprehensive and user-friendly than that of the Senate. Even here, however, using technology can not only speed up your research time, but can be a useful communications tool. *Every* member of Congress has a home page where you can review his or her record and send e-mail. You can access these through THOMAS. You should not, however, rely on e-mail to convey your lobbying message. Members themselves rarely consult their office's mailbox—this is a task for *very* junior staff. They tend to count e-mail messages rather than read them, and usually do not respond to them. For information about e-mailing congress, try INFOSEARCH's Mr. Smith E-Mails Washington. The address is, http://www.xmission.com/~insearch/washington.html.

Appendix

The Lobbying Disclosure Act of 1995

★ ★ ★ ★ ★

Senate Bill 1060
One Hundred Fourth Congress
of the United States of America
At the First Session
Begun and held at the City of Washington on Wednesday, the fourth
day of January, one thousand nine hundred and ninety-five
An Act
To provide for the disclosure of lobbying activities to influence
the Federal Government, and for other purposes.
Be it enacted by the Senate and House of Representatives of the
United States of America in Congress assembled,

Section 1: Short Title

This Act may be cited as the 'Lobbying Disclosure Act of 1995.'

Section 2: Findings

The Congress finds that: (1) responsible representative Government requires public awareness of the efforts of paid lobbyists to influence the public decision-making process in both the legislative and executive branches of the Federal Government; (2) existing lobbying disclosure statutes have been ineffective because of unclear statutory language, weak administrative and enforcement provisions, and an absence of clear guidance as to who is required to register and what they are required to disclose; and (3) the effective public disclosure of the identity and extent of the efforts of paid lobbyists to influence Federal officials in the conduct of Government actions will increase public confidence in the integrity of Government.

Section 3: Definitions

As used in this Act:

(1) **Agency:** The term 'agency' has the meaning given that term in section 551(1) of title 5, United States Code.

(2) **Client:** The term 'client' means any person or entity that employs or retains another person for financial or other compensation to conduct lobbying activities on behalf of that person or entity. A person or entity whose employees act as lobbyists on its own behalf is both a client and an employer of such employees. In the case of a coalition or association that employs or retains other persons to conduct lobbying activities, the client is the coalition or association and not its individual members.

(3) **Covered Executive Branch Official:** The term 'covered executive branch official' means: (A) the President; (B) the Vice President; (C) any officer or employee, or any other individual functioning in the capacity of such an officer or employee, in the Executive Office of the President; (D) any officer or employee serving in a position in level I, II, III, IV, or V of the Executive Schedule, as designated by statute or Executive order; (E) any member of the uniformed services whose pay grade is at or above O-7 under section 201 of title 37, United States Code; and (F) any officer or employee serving in a position of a confidential, policy-determining, policy-making, or policy-advocating character described in section 7511(b)(2) of title 5, United States Code.

(4) **Covered Legislative Branch Official:** The term 'covered legislative branch official' means: (A) a Member of Congress; (B) an elected officer of either House of Congress; (C) any employee of, or any other individual functioning in the capacity of an employee of: (i) a Member of Congress; (ii) a committee of either House of Congress; (iii) the leadership staff of the House of Representatives or the leadership staff of the Senate; (iv) a joint committee of Congress; and (v) a working group or caucus organized to provide legislative services or other assistance to Members of Congress; and (D) any other legislative branch employee serving in a position described under section 109(13) of the Ethics in Government Act of 1978 (5 U.S.C. App.).

(5) **Employee:** The term 'employee' means any individual who is an officer, employee, partner, director, or proprietor of a person or entity, but does not include: (A) independent contractors; or (B) volunteers who receive no financial or other compensation from the person or entity for their services.

(6) **Foreign Entity:** The term 'foreign entity' means a foreign principal (as defined in section 1(b) of the Foreign Agents Registration Act of 1938 (22 U.S.C. 611(b)).

(7) **Lobbying Activities:** The term 'lobbying activities' means lobbying contacts and efforts in support of such contacts, including preparation and planning ac-

tivities, research and other background work that is intended, at the time it is performed, for use in contacts, and coordination with the lobbying activities of others.

(8) **Lobbying Contact:** (A) *Definition:* The term 'lobbying contact' means any oral or written communication (including an electronic communication) to a covered executive branch official or a covered legislative branch official that is made on behalf of a client with regard to: (i) the formulation, modification, or adoption of Federal legislation (including legislative proposals); (ii) the formulation, modification, or adoption of a Federal rule, regulation, Executive order, or any other program, policy, or position of the United States Government; (iii) the administration or execution of a Federal program or policy (including the negotiation, award, or administration of a Federal contract, grant, loan, permit, or license); or (iv) the nomination or confirmation of a person for a position subject to confirmation by the Senate. (B) *Exceptions:* The term 'lobbying contact' does not include a communication that is: (i) made by a public official acting in the public official's official capacity; (ii) made by a representative of a media organization if the purpose of the communication is gathering and disseminating news and information to the public; (iii) made in a speech, article, publication or other material that is distributed and made available to the public, or through radio, television, cable television, or other medium of mass communication; (iv) made on behalf of a government of a foreign country or a foreign political party and disclosed under the Foreign Agents Registration Act of 1938 (22 U.S.C. 611 et seq.); (v) a request for a meeting, a request for the status of an action, or any other similar administrative request, if the request does not include an attempt to influence a covered executive branch official or a covered legislative branch official; (vi) made in the course of participation in an advisory committee subject to the Federal Advisory Committee Act; (vii) testimony given before a committee, subcommittee, or task force of the Congress, or submitted for inclusion in the public record of a hearing conducted by such committee, subcommittee, or task force; (viii) information provided in writing in response to an oral or written request by a covered executive branch official or a covered legislative branch official for specific information; (ix) required by subpoena, civil investigative demand, or otherwise compelled by statute, regulation, or other action of the Congress or an agency; (x) made in response to a notice in the Federal Register, Commerce Business Daily, or other similar publication soliciting communications from the public and directed to the agency official specifically designated in the notice to receive such communications; (xi) not possible to report without disclosing information, the unauthorized disclosure of which is prohibited by law; (xii) made to an official in an agency with regard to: (I) a judicial proceeding or a criminal or civil law enforcement inquiry, investigation, or proceeding; or (II) a filing or proceeding that the Government is specifically required by statute or regulation to maintain or conduct on a confidential basis, if that agency is charged with responsibility for such proceeding, inquiry, investigation, or filing; (xiii) made in compliance with written agency procedures regarding an adjudication conducted by the agency under section 554 of title 5, United States Code, or substantially similar provisions; (xiv) a written

comment filed in the course of a public proceeding or any other communication that is made on the record in a public proceeding; (xv) a petition for agency action made in writing and required to be a matter of public record pursuant to established agency procedures; (xvi) made on behalf of an individual with regard to that individual's benefits, employment, or other personal matters involving only that individual, except that this clause does not apply to any communication with: (I) a covered executive branch official, or (II) a covered legislative branch official (other than the individual's elected Members of Congress or employees who work under such Members' direct supervision), with respect to the formulation, modification, or adoption of private legislation for the relief of that individual; (xvii) a disclosure by an individual that is protected under the amendments made by the Whistleblower Protection Act of 1989, under the Inspector General Act of 1978, or under another provision of law; (xviii) made by: (I) a church, its integrated auxiliary, or a convention or association of churches that is exempt from filing a Federal income tax return under paragraph 2(A)(i) of section 6033(a) of the Internal Revenue Code of 1986, or (II) a religious order that is exempt from filing a Federal income tax return under paragraph (2)(A)(iii) of such section 6033(a); and (xix) between: (I) officials of a self-regulatory organization (as defined in section 3(a)(26) of the Securities Exchange Act) that is registered with or established by the Securities and Exchange Commission as required by that Act or a similar organization that is designated by or registered with the Commodities Future Trading Commission as provided under the Commodity Exchange Act; and (II) the Securities and Exchange Commission or the Commodities Future Trading Commission, respectively; relating to the regulatory responsibilities of such organization under that Act.

(9) **Lobbying Firm:** The term 'lobbying firm' means a person or entity that has 1 or more employees who are lobbyists on behalf of a client other than that person or entity. The term also includes a self-employed individual who is a lobbyist.

(10) **Lobbyist:** The term 'lobbyist' means any individual who is employed or retained by a client for financial or other compensation for services that include more than one lobbying contact, other than an individual whose lobbying activities constitute less than 20 percent of the time engaged in the services provided by such individual to that client over a six month period.

(11) **Media Organization:** The term 'media organization' means a person or entity engaged in disseminating information to the general public through a newspaper, magazine, other publication, radio, television, cable television, or other medium of mass communication.

(12) **Member of Congress:** The term 'Member of Congress' means a Senator or a Representative in, or Delegate or Resident Commissioner to, the Congress.

(13) **Organization:** The term 'organization' means a person or entity other than an individual.

(14) **Person or Entity:** The term 'person or entity' means any individual, corporation, company, foundation, association, labor organization, firm, partnership,

society, joint stock company, group of organizations, or State or local government.

(15) **Public Official:** The term 'public official' means any elected official, appointed official, or employee of: (A) a Federal, State, or local unit of government in the United States other than: (i) a college or university; (ii) a government-sponsored enterprise (as defined in section 3(8) of the Congressional Budget and Impoundment Control Act of 1974); (iii) a public utility that provides gas, electricity, water, or communications; (iv) a guaranty agency (as defined in section 435(j) of the Higher Education Act of 1965 (20 U.S.C. 1085(j))), including any affiliate of such an agency; or (v) an agency of any State functioning as a student loan secondary market pursuant to section 435(d)(1)(F) of the Higher Education Act of 1965 (20 U.S.C. 1085(d)(1)(F)); (B) a Government corporation (as defined in section 9101 of title 31, United States Code); (C) an organization of State or local elected or appointed officials other than officials of an entity described in clause (i), (ii), (iii), (iv), or (v) of subparagraph (A); (D) an Indian tribe (as defined in section 4(e) of the Indian Self-Determination and Education Assistance Act (25 U.S.C. 450b(e)); (E) a national or State political party or any organizational unit thereof; or (F) a national, regional, or local unit of any foreign government.

(16) **State:** The term 'State' means each of the several States, the District of Columbia, and any commonwealth, territory, or possession of the United States.

Section 4: Registration Of Lobbyists

(a) **Registration:** (1) *General Rule:* No later than 45 days after a lobbyist first makes a lobbying contact or is employed or retained to make a lobbying contact, whichever is earlier, such lobbyist (or, as provided under paragraph (2), the organization employing such lobbyist), shall register with the Secretary of the Senate and the Clerk of the House of Representatives. (2) *Employer Filing:* Any organization that has one or more employees who are lobbyists shall file a single registration under this section on behalf of such employees for each client on whose behalf the employees act as lobbyists. (3) *Exemption:* (A) *General Rule:* Notwithstanding paragraphs (1) and (2), a person or entity whose: (i) total income for matters related to lobbying activities on behalf of a particular client (in the case of a lobbying firm) does not exceed and is not expected to exceed $5,000; or (ii) total expenses in connection with lobbying activities (in the case of an organization whose employees engage in lobbying activities on its own behalf) do not exceed or are not expected to exceed $20,000, (as estimated under section 5) in the semiannual period described in section 5(a) during which the registration would be made is not required to register under subsection (a) with respect to such client. (B) *Adjustment:* The dollar amounts in subparagraph (A) shall be adjusted: (i) on January 1, 1997, to reflect changes in the Consumer Price Index (as determined by the Secretary of Labor) since the date of enactment of this Act; and (ii) on January 1 of each fourth year occurring after January 1, 1997, to reflect changes in the Consumer Price Index (as determined by the Secretary of Labor) during the preceding four-year period, rounded to the nearest $500.

(b) **Contents of Registration:** Each registration under this section shall contain: (1) the name, address, business telephone number, and principal place of business of the registrant, and a general description of its business or activities; (2) the name, address, and principal place of business of the registrant's client, and a general description of its business or activities (if different from paragraph (1)); (3) the name, address, and principal place of business of any organization, other than the client, that: (A) contributes more than $10,000 toward the lobbying activities of the registrant in a semiannual period described in section 5(a); and (B) in whole or in major part plans, supervises, or controls such lobbying activities. (4) the name, address, principal place of business, amount of any contribution of more than $10,000 to the lobbying activities of the registrant, and approximate percentage of equitable ownership in the client (if any) of any foreign entity that: (A) holds at least 20 percent equitable ownership in the client or any organization identified under paragraph (3); (B) directly or indirectly, in whole or in major part, plans, supervises, controls, directs, finances, or subsidizes the activities of the client or any organization identified under paragraph (3); or (C) is an affiliate of the client or any organization identified under paragraph (3) and has a direct interest in the outcome of the lobbying activity; (5) a statement of: (A) the general issue areas in which the registrant expects to engage in lobbying activities on behalf of the client; and (B) to the extent practicable, specific issues that have (as of the date of the registration) already been addressed or are likely to be addressed in lobbying activities; and (6) the name of each employee of the registrant who has acted or whom the registrant expects to act as a lobbyist on behalf of the client and, if any such employee has served as a covered executive branch official or a covered legislative branch official in the two years before the date on which such employee first acted (after the date of enactment of this Act) as a lobbyist on behalf of the client, the position in which such employee served.

(c) **Guidelines for Registration:** (1) *Multiple Clients:* In the case of a registrant making lobbying contacts on behalf of more than one client, a separate registration under this section shall be filed for each such client. (2) *Multiple Contacts:* A registrant who makes more than one lobbying contact for the same client shall file a single registration covering all such lobbying contacts.

(d) **Termination of Registration:** A registrant who after registration: (1) is no longer employed or retained by a client to conduct lobbying activities, and (2) does not anticipate any additional lobbying activities for such client, may so notify the Secretary of the Senate and the Clerk of the House of Representatives and terminate its registration.

Section 5: Reports by Registered Lobbyists

(a) **Semiannual Report:** No later than 45 days after the end of the semiannual period beginning on the first day of each January and the first day of July of each year in which a registrant is registered under section 4, each registrant shall file a report with the Secretary of the Senate and the Clerk of the House of Representatives on its lobbying activities during such semiannual period. A separate report shall be filed for each client of the registrant.

(b) **Contents of Report:** Each semiannual report filed under subsection (a) shall contain: (1) the name of the registrant, the name of the client, and any changes or updates to the information provided in the initial registration; (2) for each general issue area in which the registrant engaged in lobbying activities on behalf of the client during the semiannual filing period: (A) a list of the specific issues upon which a lobbyist employed by the registrant engaged in lobbying activities, including, to the maximum extent practicable, a list of bill numbers and references to specific executive branch actions; (B) a statement of the Houses of Congress and the Federal agencies contacted by lobbyists employed by the registrant on behalf of the client; (C) a list of the employees of the registrant who acted as lobbyists on behalf of the client; and (D) a description of the interest, if any, of any foreign entity identified under section 4(b)(4) in the specific issues listed under subparagraph (A); (3) in the case of a lobbying firm, a good faith estimate of the total amount of all income from the client (including any payments to the registrant by any other person for lobbying activities on behalf of the client) during the semiannual period, other than income for matters that are unrelated to lobbying activities; and (4) in the case of a registrant engaged in lobbying activities on its own behalf, a good faith estimate of the total expenses that the registrant and its employees incurred in connection with lobbying activities during the semiannual filing period.

(c) **Estimates of Income or Expenses:** For purposes of this section, estimates of income or expenses shall be made as follows: (1) Estimates of amounts in excess of $10,000 shall be rounded to the nearest $20,000. (2) In the event income or expenses do not exceed $10,000, the registrant shall include a statement that income or expenses totaled less than $10,000 for the reporting period. (3) A registrant that reports lobbying expenditures pursuant to section 6033(b)(8) of the Internal Revenue Code of 1986 may satisfy the requirement to report income or expenses by filing with the Secretary of the Senate and the Clerk of the House of Representatives a copy of the form filed in accordance with section 6033(b)(8).

Section 6: Disclosure and Enforcement

The Secretary of the Senate and the Clerk of the House of Representatives shall: (1) provide guidance and assistance on the registration and reporting requirements of this Act and develop common standards, rules, and procedures for compliance with this Act; (2) review, and, where necessary, verify and inquire to ensure the accuracy, completeness, and timeliness of registration and reports; (3) develop filing, coding, and cross-indexing systems to carry out the purpose of this Act, including: (A) a publicly available list of all registered lobbyists, lobbying firms, and their clients; and (B) computerized systems designed to minimize the burden of filing and maximize public access to materials filed under this Act; (4) make available for public inspection and copying at reasonable times the registrations and reports filed under this Act; (5) retain registrations for a period of at least 6 years after they are terminated and reports for a period of at least 6 years after they are filed; (6) compile and summarize, with respect to each semiannual period, the information contained in registrations and reports filed with respect to such period in a clear and complete manner; (7) notify any lobbyist or lobbying firm in writing that may be in noncompliance with this Act; and (8) notify the United States Attorney for the District of Columbia that a lobbyist or lobbying firm may be in noncompliance with this Act, if the registrant has been notified in writing and has failed to provide an appropriate response within 60 days after notice was given under paragraph (7).

Section 7: Penalties

Whoever knowingly fails to: (1) remedy a defective filing within 60 days after notice of such a defect by the Secretary of the Senate or the Clerk of the House of Representatives; or (2) comply with any other provision of this Act; shall, upon proof of such knowing violation by a preponderance of the evidence, be subject to a civil fine of not more than $50,000, depending on the extent and gravity of the violation.

Section 8: Rules Of Construction

(a) **Constitutional Rights:** Nothing in this Act shall be construed to prohibit or interfere with: (1) the right to petition the Government for the redress of grievances; (2) the right to express a personal opinion; or (3) the right of association, protected by the first amendment to the Constitution.

(b) **Prohibition of Activities:** Nothing in this Act shall be construed to prohibit, or to authorize any court to prohibit, lobbying activities or lobbying contacts by any person or entity, regardless of whether such person or entity is in compliance with the requirements of this Act.

(c) **Audit and Investigations:** Nothing in this Act shall be construed to grant general audit or investigative authority to the Secretary of the Senate or the Clerk of the House of Representatives.

Section 9: Amendments to the Foreign Agents Registration Act

The Foreign Agents Registration Act of 1938 (22 U.S.C. 611 et seq.) is amended: (1) in section 1: (A) by striking subsection (j); (B) in subsection (o) by striking 'the dissemination of political propaganda and any other activity which the person engaging therein believes will, or which he intends to, prevail upon, indoctrinate, convert, induce, persuade, or in any other way influence' and inserting 'any activity that the person engaging in believes will, or that the person intends to, in any way influence'; (C) in subsection (p) by striking the semicolon and inserting a period; and (D) by striking subsection (q); (2) in section 3(g) (22 U.S.C. 613(g)), by striking 'established agency proceedings, whether formal or informal.' and inserting 'judicial proceedings, criminal or civil law enforcement inquiries, investigations, or proceedings, or agency proceedings required by statute or regulation to be conducted on the record.'; (3) in section 3 (22 U.S.C. 613) by adding at the end the following: '(h) Any agent of a person described in section 1(b)(2) or an entity described in section 1(b)(3) if the agent is required to register and does register under the Lobbying Disclosure Act of 1995 in connection with the agent's representation of such person or entity.'; (4) in section 4(a) (22 U.S.C.

614(a)): (A) by striking 'political propaganda' and inserting 'informational materials'; and (B) by striking 'and a statement, duly signed by or on behalf of such an agent, setting forth full information as to the places, times, and extent of such transmittal'; (5) in section 4(b) (22 U.S.C. 614(b)): (A) in the matter preceding clause (i), by striking 'political propaganda' and inserting 'informational materials'; and (B) by striking '(i) in the form of prints, or' and all that follows through the end of the subsection and inserting 'without placing in such informational materials a conspicuous statement that the materials are distributed by the agent on behalf of the foreign principal, and that additional information is on file with the Department of Justice, Washington, District of Columbia. The Attorney General may by rule define what constitutes a conspicuous statement for the purposes of this subsection.'; (6) in section 4(c) (22 U.S.C. 614(c)), by striking 'political propaganda' and inserting 'informational materials'; (7) in section 6 (22 U.S.C. 616): (A) in subsection (a) by striking 'and all statements concerning the distribution of political propaganda'; (B) in subsection (b) by striking ', and one copy of every item of political propaganda'; and (C) in subsection (c) by striking 'copies of political propaganda,'; and (8) in section 8 (22 U.S.C. 618): (A) in subsection (a)(2) by striking 'or in any statement under section 4(a) hereof concerning the distribution of political propaganda'; and (B) by striking subsection (d).

Section 10: Amendments to the Byrd Amendment

(a) **Revised Certification Requirements:** Section 1352(b) of title 31, United States Code, is amended: (1) in paragraph (2) by striking subparagraphs (A), (B), and (C) and inserting the following: '(A) the name of any registrant under the Lobbying Disclosure Act of 1995 who has made lobbying contacts on behalf of the person with respect to that Federal contract, grant, loan, or cooperative agreement; and '(B) a certification that the person making the declaration has not made, and will not make, any payment prohibited by subsection (a).'; (2) in paragraph (3) by striking all that follows 'loan shall contain' and inserting 'the name of any registrant under the Lobbying Disclosure Act of 1995 who has made lobbying contacts on behalf of the person in connection with that loan insurance or guarantee.'; and (3) by striking paragraph (6) and redesignating paragraph (7) as paragraph (6).

(b) **Removal of Obsolete Reporting Requirement:** Section 1352 of title 31, United States Code, is further amended: (1) by striking subsection (d); and (2) by redesignating subsections (e), (f), (g), and (h) as subsections (d), (e), (f), and (g), respectively.

Section 11: Repeal of Certain Lobbying Provisions

(a) **Repeal of the Federal Regulation of Lobbying Act:** The Federal Regulation of Lobbying Act (2 U.S.C. 261 et seq.) is repealed.

(b) **Repeal of Provisions Relating to Housing Lobbyist Activities:** (1) Section 13 of the Department of Housing and Urban Development Act (42 U.S.C. 3537b) is repealed. (2) Section 536(d) of the Housing Act of 1949 (42 U.S.C. 1490p(d)) is repealed.

Section 12: Conforming Amendments to Other Statutes

(a) **Amendment to Competitiveness Policy Council Act:** Section 5206(e) of the Competitiveness Policy Council Act (15 U.S.C. 4804(e)) is amended by inserting 'or a lobbyist for a foreign entity (as the terms 'lobbyist' and 'foreign entity' are defined under section 3 of the Lobbying Disclosure Act of 1995)' after 'an agent for a foreign principal'.

(b) **Amendments to Title 18, United States Code:** Section 219(a) of title 18, United States Code, is amended: (1) by inserting 'or a lobbyist required to register under the Lobbying Disclosure Act of 1995 in connection with the representation of a foreign entity, as defined in section 3(6) of that Act' after 'an agent of a foreign principal required to register under the Foreign Agents Registration Act of 1938'; and (2) by striking out ', as amended,'.

(c) **Amendment to Foreign Service Act of 1980:** Section 602(c) of the Foreign Service Act of 1980 (22 U.S.C. 4002(c)) is amended by inserting 'or a lobbyist for a foreign entity (as defined in section 3(6) of the Lobbying Disclosure Act of 1995)' after 'an agent of a foreign principal (as defined by section 1(b) of the Foreign Agents Registration Act of 1938)'.

Section 13: Severability

If any provision of this Act, or the application thereof, is held invalid, the validity of the remainder of this Act and the application of such provision to other persons and circumstances shall not be affected thereby.

Section 14: Identification of Clients and Covered Officials

(a) **Oral Lobbying Contacts:** Any person or entity that makes an oral lobbying contact with a covered legislative branch official or a covered executive branch official shall, on the request of the official at the time of the lobbying contact: (1) state whether the person or entity is registered under this Act and identify the client on whose behalf the lobbying contact is made; and (2) state whether such client is a foreign entity and identify any foreign entity required to be disclosed under section 4(b)(4) that has a direct interest in the outcome of the lobbying activity.

(b) **Written Lobbying Contacts:** Any person or entity registered under this Act that makes a written lobbying contact (including an electronic communication) with a covered legislative branch official or a covered executive branch official shall: (1) if the client on whose behalf the lobbying contact was made is a foreign entity, identify such client, state that the client is considered a foreign entity under this Act, and state whether the person making the lobbying contact is registered on behalf of that client under section 4; and (2) identify any other foreign entity identified pursuant to section 4(b)(4) that has a direct interest in the outcome of the lobbying activity.

(c) **Identification as Covered Official:** Upon request by a person or entity making a lobbying contact, the individual who is contacted or the office employing that individual shall indicate whether or not the individual is a covered legislative branch official or a covered executive branch official.

Section 15: Estimates Based on Tax Reporting System

(a) **Entities Covered by Section 6033(b) of The Internal Revenue Code of 1986:** A registrant that is required to report and does report lobbying expenditures pursuant to section 6033(b)(8) of the Internal Revenue Code of 1986 may: (1) make a good faith estimate (by category of dollar value) of applicable amounts that would be required to be disclosed under such section for the appropriate semiannual period to meet the requirements of sections 4(a)(3) and 5(b)(4); and (2) in lieu of using the definition of 'lobbying activities' in section 3(7) of this Act, consider as lobbying activities only those activities that are influencing legislation as defined in section 4911(d) of the Internal Revenue Code of 1986.

(b) **Entities Covered by Section 162(e) of The Internal Revenue Code of 1986:** A registrant that is subject to section 162(e) of the Internal Revenue Code of 1986 may: (1) make a good faith estimate (by category of dollar value) of applicable amounts that would not be deductible pursuant to such section for the appropriate semiannual period to meet the requirements of sections 4(a)(3) and 5(b)(4); and (2) in lieu of using the definition of 'lobbying activities' in section 3(7) of this Act, consider as lobbying activities only those activities, the costs of which are not deductible pursuant to section 162(e) of the Internal Revenue Code of 1986.

(c) **Disclosure of Estimate:** Any registrant that elects to make estimates required by this Act under the procedures authorized by subsection (a) or (b) for reporting or threshold purposes shall: (1) inform the Secretary of the Senate and the Clerk of the House of Representatives that the registrant has elected to make its estimates under such procedures; and (2) make all such estimates, in a given calendar year, under such procedures.

(d) **Study:** Not later than March 31, 1997, the Comptroller General of the United States shall review reporting by registrants under subsections (a) and (b) and report to the Congress: (1) the differences between the definition of 'lobbying activities' in section 3(7) and the definitions of 'lobbying expenditures', 'influencing legislation', and related terms in sections 162(e) and 4911 of the Internal Revenue Code of 1986, as each are implemented by regulations; (2) the impact that any such differences may have on filing and reporting under this Act pursuant to this subsection; and (3) any changes to this Act or to the appropriate sections of the Internal Revenue Code of 1986 that the Comptroller General may recommend to harmonize the definitions.

Section 16: Repeal of The Ramspeck Act

(a) **Repeal:** Subsection (c) of section 3304 of title 5, United States Code, is repealed.

(b) **Redesignation:** Subsection (d) of section 3304 of title 5, United States Code, is redesignated as subsection (c).

(c) **Effective Date:** The repeal and amendment made by this section shall take effect two years after the date of the enactment of this Act.

Section 17: Excepted Service and Other Experience Considerations for Competitive Service Appointments

(a) **In General:** Section 3304 of title 5, United States Code (as amended by section 2 of this Act) is further amended by adding at the end thereof the following new subsection: '(d) The Office of Personnel Management shall promulgate regulations on the manner and extent that experience of an individual in a position other than the competitive service, such as the excepted service (as defined under section 2103) in the legislative or judicial branch, or in any private or non-profit enterprise, may be considered in making appointments to a position in the competitive service (as defined under section 2102). In promulgating such regulations OPM shall not grant any preference based on the fact of service in the legislative or judicial branch. The regulations shall be consistent with the principles of equitable competition and merit based appointments.'

(b) **Effective Date:** The amendment made by this section shall take effect two years after the date of the enactment of this Act, except the Office of Personnel Management shall: (1) conduct a study on excepted service considerations for competitive service appointments relating to such amendment; and (2) take all necessary actions for the regulations described under such amendment to take effect as final regulations on the effective date of this section.

Section 18: Exempt Organizations

An organization described in section 501(c)(4) of The Internal Revenue Code of 1986 which engages in lobbying activities shall not be eligible for the receipt of Federal funds constituting an award, grant, contract, loan, or any other form.

Section 19: Amendment to the Foreign Agents Registration Act (P.L. 75-583)

Strike section 11 of the Foreign Agents Registration Act of 1938, as amended, and insert in lieu thereof the following: 'Section 11. Reports to the Congress: The Attorney General shall every six months report to the Congress concerning administration of this Act, including registrations filed pursuant to the Act, and the nature, sources and content of political propaganda disseminated and distributed.'

Section 20: Disclosure of the Value of Assets Under the Ethics in Government Act of 1978

(a) **Income:** Section 102(a)(1)(B) of the Ethics in Government Act of 1978 is amended: (1) in clause (vii) by striking 'or'; and (2) by striking clause (viii) and inserting the following: '(viii) greater than $1,000,000 but not more than $5,000,000, or '(ix) greater than $5,000,000.'

(b) **Assets and Liabilities:** Section 102(d)(1) of the Ethics in Government Act of 1978 is amended: (1) in subparagraph (F) by striking 'and'; and (2) by striking subparagraph (G) and inserting the following: '(G) greater than $1,000,000 but not more than $5,000,000; '(H) greater than $5,000,000 but not more than

$25,000,000; '(I) greater than $25,000,000 but not more than $50,000,000; and '(J) greater than $50,000,000.'

(c) **Exception:** Section 102(e)(1) of the Ethics in Government Act of 1978 is amended by adding after subparagraph (E) the following: '(F) For purposes of this section, categories with amounts or values greater than $1,000,000 set forth in sections 102(a)(1)(B) and 102(d)(1) shall apply to the income, assets, or liabilities of spouses and dependent children only if the income, assets, or liabilities are held jointly with the reporting individual. All other income, assets, or liabilities of the spouse or dependent children required to be reported under this section in an amount or value greater than $1,000,000 shall be categorized only as an amount or value greater than $1,000,000.'

Section 21: Ban on Trade Representative Representing or Advising Foreign Entities

(a) **Representing After Service:** Section 207(f)(2) of title 18, United States Code, is amended by: (1) inserting 'or Deputy United States Trade Representative' after 'is the United States Trade Representative'; and (2) striking 'within 3 years' and inserting 'at any time'.

(b) **Limitation on Appointment as United States Trade Representative and Deputy United States Trade Representative:** Section 141(b) of the Trade Act of 1974 (19 U.S.C. 2171(b)) is amended by adding at the end the following new paragraph: '(3) Limitation on Appointments: A person who has directly represented, aided, or advised a foreign entity (as defined by section 207(f)(3) of title 18, United States Code) in any trade negotiation, or trade dispute, with the United States may not be appointed as United States Trade Representative or as a Deputy United States Trade Representative.'

(c) **Effective Date:** The amendments made by this section shall apply with respect to an individual appointed as United States Trade Representative or as a Deputy United States Trade Representative on or after the date of enactment of this Act.

Section 22: Financial Disclosure of Interest in Qualified Blind Trust

(a) **In General:** Section 102(a) of the Ethics in Government Act of 1978 is amended by adding at the end thereof the following: '(8) The category of the total cash value of any interest of the reporting individual in a qualified blind trust, unless the trust instrument was executed prior to July 24, 1995 and precludes the beneficiary from receiving information on the total cash value of any interest in the qualified blind trust.'

(b) **Conforming Amendment:** Section 102(d)(1) of the Ethics in Government Act of 1978 is amended by striking 'and (5) and inserting '(5), and (8)'.

(c) **Effective Date:** The amendment made by this section shall apply with respect to reports filed under title I of the Ethics in Government Act of 1978 for calendar year 1996 and thereafter.

Section 23: Sense of the Senate that Lobbying Expenses Should Remain Nondeductible

(a) **Findings:** The Senate finds that ordinary Americans generally are not allowed to deduct the costs of communicating with their elected representatives.

(b) **Sense of the Senate:** It is the sense of the Senate that lobbying expenses should not be tax deductible.

Section 24: Effective Dates

(a) Except as otherwise provided in this section, this Act and the amendments made by this Act shall take effect on January 1, 1996. (b) The repeals and amendments made under sections 9, 10, 11, and 12 shall take effect as provided under subsection (a), except that such repeals and amendments: (1) shall not affect any proceeding or suit commenced before the effective date under subsection (a), and in all such proceedings or suits, proceedings shall be had, appeals taken, and judgments rendered in the same manner and with the same effect as if this Act had not been enacted; and (2) shall not affect the requirements of Federal agencies to compile, publish, and retain information filed or received before the effective date of such repeals and amendments.

Speaker of the House of Representatives
Vice President of the United States and
President of the Senate

Bibliography

American Enterprise Institute for Public Policy Research. *Lobbying: A Constitutionally Protected Right.* Washington, D.C. 1977.

Barnes, Robert A., and others. *The Washington Lobby.* Washington, D.C.: Congressional Quarterly, Inc. 1971.

Gallagher, Janne G. *Lobbying and Political Activity Restrictions for Federal Grantees and Contractors.* 1995. Electronic book available at http://rtk.net/www/las/galrpt.html.

Howe, Russell Warren and Sara Hays Trott. *The Power Peddlers.* Garden City, N.Y.: Doubleday. 1977.

Investigation of Lobbying Activities Report. Pursuant to House Resolution 288. Washington, D.C.: United States Printing Office. 1936.

Lobbying and the Law. Berkeley, CA: University of California Press. 1964.

Lobbying Congress. American Civil Liberties Union. 1995. Electronic book available at http://www.aclu.org/congress/lobbying.html.

Manual of Legislative Techniques. Chicago: National Association of Bar Executives. 1975.

Martin, Ryan, Haley & Associates. *Campaign Contributions and Lobbying Laws* (condensed). Arlington, VA. 1978.

Neale, Reg. *Lobbying/Advocacy Techniques.* 1994. Electronic book available at http://muon.que.com/space/guidelines/lobby_techniquesfaq.html.

Ozols, Aldis. *How to Lobby Politicians.* 1996. Electronic book available at http://www.ocemail.com.au.html.

Pressures Upon Congress: Legislation by Lobby. Woodbury, N.Y.: Barron's Educational Series, Inc. 1973.

Segell, J. Peter. A Summary of Lobbying Disclosure Laws and Regulations in the Fifty States. Washington, D.C.: Plus Publications. 1979.

Shaw, Rancy. *The Acitivist's Guide.* Berkeley, CA: University of California Press. 1976.

Special Committee on Election Laws. *Campaign and Lobbying Law Handbook.* Los Angeles: Los Angeles County Bar Association. 1976.

Webster, George D. *Associations and Lobbying Regulation: A Guide for Non-Profit Organizations.* Washington, D.C.: Chamber of Commerce of the United States, Association Division. 1977.

Willett, Jr., Edward F., Esq. *How Our Laws Are Made.* 1989. Electronic book available at http://www.loc.gov.html.

Wittenberg, Ernest and Elizabeth. *How to Win in Washington.* Cambridge, MA: Blackwell Publishers. 1994.

Wolpe, Bruce C. *Lobbying Congress.* Washington, D.C.: Congressional Quarterly, Inc. 1990.

Zuckerman, Edward. *Directory of Lobbyists, Lawyers and Interest Groups.* Rockville, MD: Amward Publications, Inc. 1993.

Donald E. deKieffer has practiced international trade law and government relations in Washington, D.C. for twenty-five years. He has testified more than thirty times before congressional committees and has been a registered lobbyist for numerous organizations. He lives in McLean, Virginia.

Index